SCRATCH MY BELLY
& I'LL FOLLOW YOU ANYWHERE

A Collection of Dog Tales:
Going from Woe to Woof

Edited by
Jean Tennant

Shapato Publishing, LLC

Everly, Iowa

Published by: Shapato Publishing, LLC
                PO Box 476
                Everly, Iowa 51338

ISBN-13: 978-0692580929
ISBN-10: 0692580921

Library of Congress Control Number: 2012921097

Front Cover: Ike. Photo courtesy of Stephanie O'Brien
Back Cover: Boomer. Photo courtesy of Stephanie O'Brien

First Printing November 2015

"If there are no dogs in Heaven, then when I die I want to go where they went." *Will Rogers*

This book is dedicated to the memory of Grover Reiser.
He is greatly missed by his wife, his extended family, his many friends,
and by his little white terrier, Kirby Puckett.

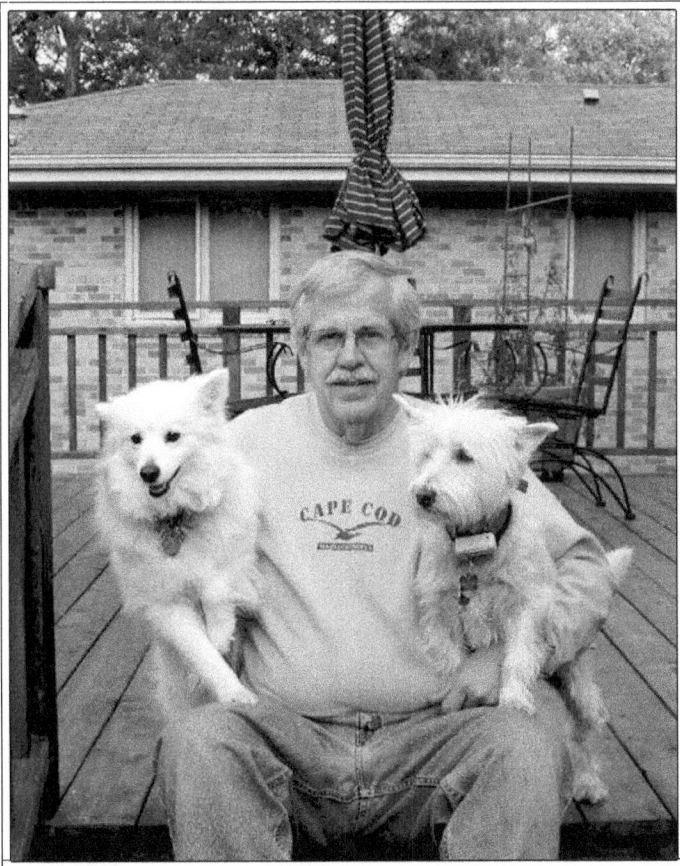

Grover Reiser,
with Dakota & Kirby

TABLE OF CONTENTS

WHEN KIRBY WAS LOST... AND FOUND 13
Grover Reiser

SPECIAL NEEDS NELLIE 19
Charlene Yager

PEANUT 25
Beverly A. VanEman

STRANDED IN A BLIZZARD 31
Fred E. Oberski

RESCUED TWICE 37
Sarah Simmons

HE RESCUED ME 43
Michelle Kuemper

ADOPTION DAY 49
Mary Ellen Trombley

JAKE, A REASON TO LIVE 53
Carolyn Rohrbaugh

BABY JOEY COMES HOME 59
Phillip M. Ritenour

EMILIE'S REVENGE 65
Susan Dunn Schmid

GORDY AND THE SQUIRRELS 71
Gray DeMotta

ON A LONELY ROAD 79
Josie Rivara

HIS NAME WAS SWISHER 85
Arlene Young

KONG TIME 91
Bonnie Boeck Ewoldt

THIRD TIME'S A CHARM 95
R'becca Groff

JUNIPER'S STORY 103
Darwin Hagarty

REMEMBERING CHIEF 111
Janet Branson

A TALE OF TWO DOGS 117
Susan Chappelear

A PIECE OF OUR LIVES' DELIGHT 123
Evan Guilford-Blake

ACE 131
Lori Taylor

SEND US YOUR STORY 139

"You can say any foolish thing to a dog, and the dog will give you a look that says, 'Wow, you're right! I never would've thought of that!'" ~ Dave Barry

SCRATCH MY BELLY

& I'LL FOLLOW YOU ANYWHERE

A Collection of Dog Tales:
Going from Woe to Woof

Kirby

WHEN KIRBY WAS LOST... AND FOUND

Grover Reiser

Kirby came to me and my wife when he was six months old. His full name was Kirby Puckett, so named because he was short and fast. We fell in love with the energetic Westie mix that barked at squirrels and chased rabbits every chance he got. To keep him in the yard, we had an underground fence installed—Kirby wore a collar that would buzz, then give him a mild shock if he tried to cross it. But Jean hated the collar so we always kept it at a low setting. And Kirby, being a smart guy, figured out that if he ran through it fast enough he'd get only a mild buzz for a couple of seconds. Neighborhood temptations were sometimes just too much, and it wasn't unusual for him to blow the fence.

So when he came up missing from the yard one Labor Day afternoon when he was four years old, we naturally assumed he was nearby and went looking for him. Usually we located him pretty quickly. Sometimes one of the neighbors would bring him back. Everyone knew Kirby.

But this time was different. After walking around the neighborhood for a while, we got in the car. Two hours later we were very worried. It was also getting late, and I had to leave soon for my job driving truck. I hated to leave Jean with the problem of finding Kirby, but by then she'd already made up a flier with his photo and our phone number. She emailed it to everyone we knew within a twenty-five-mile radius, and printed copies to put on the bulletin board at the post office.

The next day Jean also had to go to work, but during her breaks she called the local shelters, KICD radio station in nearby Spencer, and several area veterinarians. Word was getting out, but still no Kirby. I called her cell phone regularly for updates. Wednesday and Thursday came with no word on our little dog, and we were miserable. When I got home late Thursday night, Jean said, "I'd rather find his dead body on the road somewhere than to never know what happened to him." I agreed. Our worst fear was that he was trapped somewhere and suffering.

At 6:30 AM on Friday, as Jean was getting ready to leave for work, the phone rang. "Who's calling this time of the morning?" I said, and Jean immediately replied, "It's someone calling about Kirby."

On the phone was Jean's sister Donna, who lived just a few miles away, telling us that she had forwarded the flier to all the "animal people" she knew. She'd gotten a call from Val, a dog groomer friend of hers in a town more than forty miles away. Just the day before, Val had explained, she'd heard from Rhonda, a friend of hers in yet another small town, who said a little white dog with no collar had shown up at her farmhouse. Since the dog looked as though it had been recently groomed, she wondered if Val knew whose it might be.

Val had called Donna and said, "I think I know where your sister's dog is!" Now Donna was calling us with the good news. She gave us Val's phone number. A few minutes later Val gave us Rhonda's phone number. We called.

"I'm so sorry to tell you this," Rhonda said, "but he was following our car when we left to go somewhere last night and we haven't seen him since."

So close, only to be disappointed again!

I decided to drive there anyway, on the off chance I'd find Kirby wandering the roads. It was better than sitting around doing nothing.

An hour later I was at Rhonda's farmhouse, where she greeted me with some exciting news. There'd been a voice message on her answering machine, she told me, from a neighbor, a young man named Luke, saying he'd picked up a small white dog running down the middle of the road in the rain. Since it hadn't been far from her place, he wondered if she knew whose dog it was. He'd picked the dog up, his message continued, taken it home, fed it, made a bed for it in the laundry room, and would be taking it to the veterinarian in the next town this morning. She could pick the dog up there if it was hers.

Rhonda told me where she worked, and asked that I let her know if this turned out to be my dog. Thanking her, I left to get Kirby.

I arrived at the vet's office just as a pickup was pulling into the parking lot. A young man was driving, and on the passenger seat next to him I saw... Kirby. He was looking out the window on the other side and hadn't yet seen me.

I got out of my car and hurried to the pickup. "That's my dog!" I said, overcome with joy.

Kirby's head whipped around. He spotted me. Legs churning a hundred miles an hour, he scrambled over the young man—who threw up his arms and said "Whoa!"—to the open driver's side window. I lifted Kirby out of the pickup. He buried his head under my arm as I hugged him close to me.

Luke, the Good Samaritan who'd picked up a little dog in the rain, was laughing. "He didn't like me too much, but he sure does like you!" I tried to offer him the cash reward we had offered in the fliers, but he refused to take it.

Kirby and I left. I called Jean and gave her the good news, then drove to her office. She came outside to give some hugs of her own and share in the reunion. Kirby was beside himself with joy at the sight of her, but a short while later he was even happier to be home.

We'll never know how Kirby ended up where he did; we can only speculate. He'd been wearing two collars when he went missing—the one with his tags, and the second collar for the underground fence. Both were gone when he'd appeared at Rhonda's farmhouse the next day, nearly forty miles away. He didn't take his collars off himself, and he didn't get that far from home in such a short time by himself. He had to have been picked up, probably in or near our neighborhood, and driven to where he was dropped off.

Maybe, once out of town, whoever had him took a closer look at his tags and noticed that one of them indicated he was micro-chipped, which would have identified him as being lost. Maybe whoever had him had decided then that it was time to cut him loose.

The next day, when Jean put him in the car to take him with her to run some errands, Kirby immediately went to the floor of the car and huddled there, trembling. She called me over to see. We wondered if whoever had picked him up had shoved him to the floor and told him to stay there so he wouldn't be seen. Again, we'll probably never know.

What we *do* know is that a wide circle of people, and a rather convoluted set of circumstances, made it possible for Kirby to be returned to us. And we will be forever grateful to the kind strangers who took in a little lost dog and helped him find his way home.

After a long illness, **Grover Reiser** passed away at his home in Everly, Iowa. While he was ill, Kirby stayed close by his side, offering comfort and love as only a dog can.

Suzanne & Nellie
Photo Courtesy of Charlene Yager

SPECIAL NEEDS NELLIE

Charlene Yager

"Hi, Nellie. Hi, Nellie. How are you today? Are you coming home with me today?" Suzanne said, petting the little dog's brown and white fur. Suzanne had been repeating this for the past few weeks, every time I took her to my friend Marcia's house.

Marcia fostered animals for two area shelters. Her home always had four or five cats and at least a couple of dogs. Though Suzanne had always enjoyed visiting Marcia's house and playing with the ever-changing menagerie, she understood they were not hers to take.

Our daughter Suzanne was born with Down syndrome. She was our third child, our baby, and our only girl after two sons, Tim and Adam. There was never any question that she would stay home with us and remain a part of our family, though my husband's elderly aunt had assumed at first that we would have our daughter institutionalized. I was shocked by what seemed a heartless suggestion, but my husband pointed out that his aunt, at age 89, was of a different generation.

From the start, Suzanne brought joy to our lives. Potty trained by the time she was two, she went to preschool with children her own age and learned to write the alphabet and her name. By first grade she could read, though she would always lag behind her peers in that area. She loved to dance and was a gifted mimic. Her big brothers were protective of her, but being eight and seven years older respectively, they were never in the same school she attended, so she would take the school bus home on her own.

We never learned what happened to change Suzanne's sunny disposition when she was ten years old. It didn't happen overnight, but gradually she began to withdraw. We spoke to her teachers, wondering if there was a bully at school or on the bus. Everyone insisted that wasn't the case. Tim had graduated from high school and was attending the local community college. His classes were such that he was able to play private detective. For several weeks he shadowed Suzanne, following the bus to her school in the mornings and home in the afternoons, staying far enough back to watch without anyone being aware of him. He also made spot checks during the day, when the children were playing outside. He saw no signs of bullying.

But Suzanne had lost that spark we'd always loved. Maybe it was something as simple as reaching the age where she finally understood she would never be like the other kids. The last thing we needed was the added responsibility of a dog. Then Suzanne met Nellie.

Nellie was a five-year-old Pug whose hind leg had been removed due to a nasty infection caused by the barbed wire she'd been tangled in when picked up as a stray. Though her owners had been found, they'd signed her over to the shelter rather than pay for her considerable medical bills. Most dogs get along quite well when they lose a leg. But because Pugs are naturally bow-legged, Nellie had balance problems. She hobbled along awkwardly, her comically wide eyes looking sad. Maybe that's what caught Suzanne's attention. Whatever it was, from the moment she first met Nellie, she made it her job to shower Nellie with affection. Suzanne started begging to go visit Nellie. Marcia told me the dog knew the sound of our car in the driveway, and would brighten and hop three-legged to the door to greet us.

After about a month of this, Adam, a senior in high school, accompanied us to Marcia's house. He took one look at Suzanne and Nellie together and said, "Oh, are you kidding me? Mom, you don't seriously think we aren't taking this dog home?"

Everyone was staring at me—Marcia, Adam, Suzanne and Nellie. I was clearly outvoted.

So Nellie moved in. Because Suzanne's bed was too high for the dog to jump up onto, Tim and Adam built a set of carpeted steps for her to use. Nellie and Suzanne slept curled up together every night. As Nellie adjusted to the loss of her leg her balance improved and the three of us went on walks together. Sometimes we'd go to the park, where Suzanne would very somberly tell the story of Nellie's injury to the other children who gathered around. I usually just sat back on a bench, letting Suzanne and Nellie enjoy the limelight.

Dog and girl came out of their shells, each guided by the other. When it was time for Suzanne to come home from school, Nellie would be at the front window, flat nose pressed to the glass until she saw the bus. Then her whole body would begin wiggling so much that she had trouble staying upright, and I'd open the front door to watch her dart outside to the edge of the yard. Suzanne would jump from the bus and cover her dog with hugs and kisses until they finally came inside together.

Suzanne, now in middle school, has resumed many of the activities she used to enjoy—being in school plays, acting as playground monitor for the smaller children—but her greatest joy is always coming home to Nellie. Maybe there is a clue as to what caused Suzanne's sadness a few years back, because more than once I've heard her say to Nellie, "It's okay if you're different, Nellie-Belly. I'm different too. We still love each other."

They sure do.

Charlene Yager is a mixed-media artist from San Jose, California. She has begun incorporating images of Suzanne and Nellie in her work, using their bond as an expression of joy and acceptance.

Peanut & Bev
Photo Courtesy of Beverly A. VanEman

PEANUT

Beverly A. VanEman

"A dachshund is a half-dog high and a dog-and-a-half long."
– H.L. Mencken

It all began with a want ad in our local Montevideo, Minnesota newspaper:

FREE to good home.
Standard-sized, smooth-haired red dachshund.
Good with kids.

After a quick phone call we found that the dachshund did not factor into the family's coming move, and they really wanted a good home for him. We had already decided we would get a dog only when we found one that needed a home. Perfect! We headed for town.

When we picked up the little dog he looked up at my husband, Denny, and snuggled right in next to him. He even tried to climb onto Denny's lap to help drive home. It was like a special moment between these new best friends. He was one happy dog, and now he had four new best friends to lavish with his love.

His name was Peanut. He was lively, playful, and very devoted. Our two young daughters, Paris and Heidi, loved him immediately. They played with him for hours and he took turns sleeping every other night with one girl or the other. Sometimes it was almost seemed as though he felt he'd made a mistake. Maybe he had slept with Paris last night and it was Heidi's turn. We would hear him jump down from one bed and jump into bed with the other girl. He was sweet as sugar and extremely loveable.

Peanut's body language sometimes gave the impression that he did not know or care about his relatively small size. The farm animals ranged from hogs to chickens and even a horse. He didn't care what situation might arise, he fit right in and, as necessary, made them fit in as well! Maybe it was his wagging tail that gave him the attitude.

The dachshund is bred to scent, chase and flush out badgers and other burrow-dwelling animals. Their deep chests give them increased lung capacity. Why should we be surprised that sometimes he would go to the fields with Denny and then disappear? Our farm had drainage ditches, and more than once all we could see was his tail sticking out of a burrow, hot after something. Eventually he would come out with that "you win" pose and head for the house.

His increased lung capacity was most evident when we took him to Lake Okoboji, in Iowa. Peanuts was obsessed!

He'd dive right into the water until we could no longer see him. We would start to worry that he had been under water far too long and needed to come up for air. Panic would begin to set in and then there it was: the very tip of his wagging tail, the first sign of him. No rescue was necessary. He would purposefully go under to get the biggest rock he could break loose and wrap his jaws around. Then he used his short, muscular legs and all his strength to pull that rock to the beach, backing up all the way.

When Minnesota became a frozen wonderland Peanut loved playing in the snow. He had such a playful demeanor, and would run after the snowballs we threw only to watch them disappear into the white stuff. He didn't care. He was having so much fun, and he continued to play. Once, during a blizzard, our friends came to stay with us because their furnace had gone out. Their three children loved Peanut as well, and it was such fun! When their son Scott settled in for the night he wanted Peanut to sleep with him. He called to Peanut and got him to burrow down into the sleeping bag with him.

I can still hear his dad, Wayne, say, "Don't zip that up too far or you might have something more than Peanut in there by morning."

When we would take a road trip, we never knew how crowded the car might be. Sometimes, Peanut sat upright next to Denny, who was driving. Or he might spread out horizontally as much as he could. Sometimes he wore the sunglasses Denny put on him, and he always barked when the station attendant pumped the gas.

Peanut loved to go camping with us and would do whatever we wanted to do. He was a beam of light in our lives. The little dog brought out the best in each of us and was one of our greatest companions.

Years have passed since those happy days when our girls were young. Many of our family friends have passed as well, leaving pleasant memories. They belong to each of us in our own way. I tell my grandchildren that my home is filled with many happy memories, treasures only in my heart. Now it is time for them to go out and make their own memories. I hope that someday their memories will include a dog as special as Peanut.

His wagging tail seemed to tell us how much he loved us. He seemed to say, "I love you more than life itself, please love me back." And we did.

After having many interesting chapters in her life, **Beverly A. VanEman** is retired. The best chapters involve her husband Dennis and their lovely family. They have two grown daughters, Paris and Heidi—who are both married to Jims—and four grandchildren: Drew, Natalie, Ethan and Colby. They all live in the Portland, Oregon area. After moving to Oregon they owned and operated a real estate company. They love Silverton, a rural community south of Portland.

Peanut & Family
Photo courtesy of Beverly A. VanEman

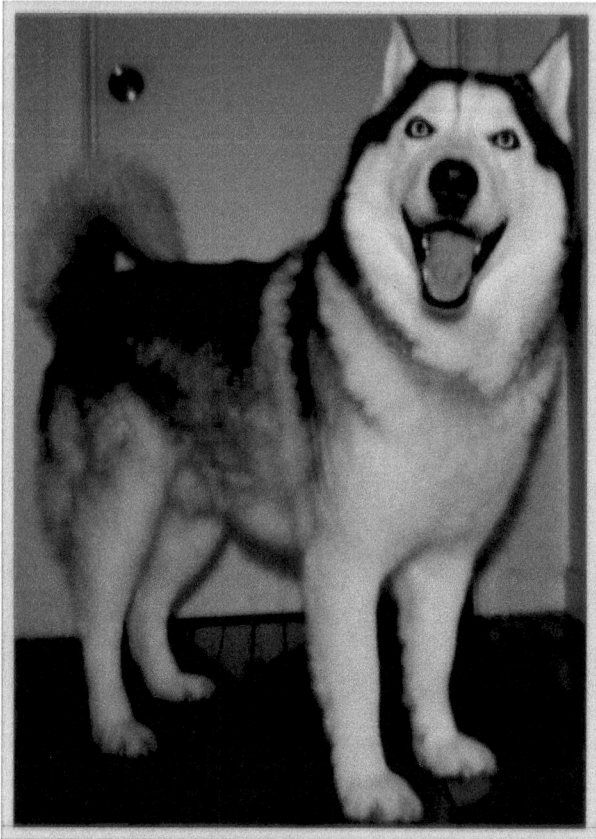

Rocco
Photo Courtesy of Fred E. Oberski

STRANDED IN A BLIZZARD

Fred E. Oberski

Visibility was poor and the temperature had dropped to nearly zero, with a wind-chill factor of minus ten degrees, but I kept driving, determined to get home. Foolish? Definitely. I'd heard all the reports; drivers were advised to stay off the roads until morning. But I'd lived in Northern Minnesota nearly all of my life. I knew how to drive in the snow. And with my dependable four-wheel-drive Ford pickup, a little bad weather didn't scare me.

On the seat next to me was Rocco, curled in a ball, sound asleep. He wasn't worried, so why should I be? Rocco was a beautiful black and white Husky with startlingly blue eyes, all of a hundred and twenty-five pounds, at least half of it seemingly made up of thick, double-layered fur. He looked like he'd be comfortable in the lead position, pulling a sled in an Iditarod race. When he wasn't sleeping, that is.

Rocco had come to me just a year earlier. He'd been picked up by animal control, thin, obviously neglected, and

31

skittish around people. They figured he'd been dumped, who knew for what reason. At the time my younger sister Georgia was working part time at the shelter, and she told me about the young Husky.

"He's a beautiful dog," she told me when she stopped at the house one day on her way home from work. "Even dirty and skinny, you can see he'll clean up good. There's really something special about him."

Georgia often told me about the animals that came into the shelter, and never failed to tell me I needed a dog. She had two dogs and three cats—all rescues—and she believed I was living a sad and lonely life without a pet to keep me company.

"I'm on the road a lot," I reminded her.

"That's the good thing about a dog. You can take it with you."

"Only if the weather's perfect. I couldn't leave a dog in the car if it were too hot or too cold." I worked as a medical supply rep for a nationwide company, a job that had me traveling at least two weeks out of four, covering three states.

Georgia was persistent, I had to give her that. She gave me regular updates on the Husky's condition. He was eating well and putting on weight. As he learned to trust the veterinarians, employees and volunteers at the shelter, his wariness had vanished. Still, I resisted. Then she pulled out the big guns—she showed up at my house with the dog.

She was right, he was gorgeous, with a broad chest and eyes that looked right into me and grabbed my heart. I was putty in his paws.

The next day I went to the shelter and filled out the adoption application.

Rocco went everywhere with me, even on my travels for work. He was an easy-going companion, and something of an ambassador for the medical supply business. My regular customers kept treats on hand for him, and if I did happen to leave him back at the motel, they'd always ask, "Where's Rocco?"

Now, headed for home, the tires slipped on the icy road. Rocco lifted his head and yawned. He gave me a look that seemed to ask "Are we there yet?"

At that moment the pickup hit a drift, and the steering wheel was jerked from my grasp. Before I could regain control we bounced into a ditch, out the other side and down a steep hill. It all happened so fast. I was wearing my seatbelt but Rocco was tossed to the floor of the pickup, which came to rest on its right side, wheels spinning.

Next thing I knew, Rocco was licking my face. I hadn't even realized I'd lost consciousness. I managed to unfasten my seatbelt and push open the driver's side door. The snow was coming down heavier, and I hadn't seen another vehicle for a while. We would have to climb up the embankment to the road, but I was more banged up than I'd first realized, and doubted I would make it.

I tried to start the pickup, but there was nothing. With no heat, the inside of the cab was growing colder by the second. I pulled the door closed again to keep what little heat we had from escaping. There was a blanket and small emergency kit behind the seats. The blanket offered some protection, but I doubted it would be enough. I had a flashlight, and as the cold seeped into my bones I pointed the beam upwards and clicked it off and on in a Morse Code SOS pattern until the batteries began to weaken.

My eyes closed, and I must have dozed. I was no longer as cold as I had been. Rocco had positioned himself right on top of me, his thick fur acting as a layer of insulation between me and the elements. The heat he gave off was better than any blanket.

When I opened my eyes again, the snow had stopped and it was getting light. I would have to try again to climb out of the pickup. As soon as I opened the door, Rocco was out. The snow was up to his chest, but his strong legs took him up the embankment with ease, and within minutes he had reached the top.

I was rescued because Rocco stood in the middle of the road until a car came along and was forced to stop. Later I learned that my pickup, covered in snow, was nearly invisible from the road.

My right arm was broken, possibly as a result of instinctively bracing it against the dash when the pickup had tumbled out of control. I also had some cracked ribs and

34

assorted bruises. But it could have been so much worse. I'm sure I wouldn't have survived the frigid night without Rocco to keep me warm.

My sister had said there was something special about him. He showed us both how right she was.

Fred E. Oberski continues to take Rocco on his medical-supply rounds, and has added Rocco's name to his business cards. "Stranded in a Blizzard" is his first published work, though he is currently writing a collection of stories about his many adventures with Rocco.

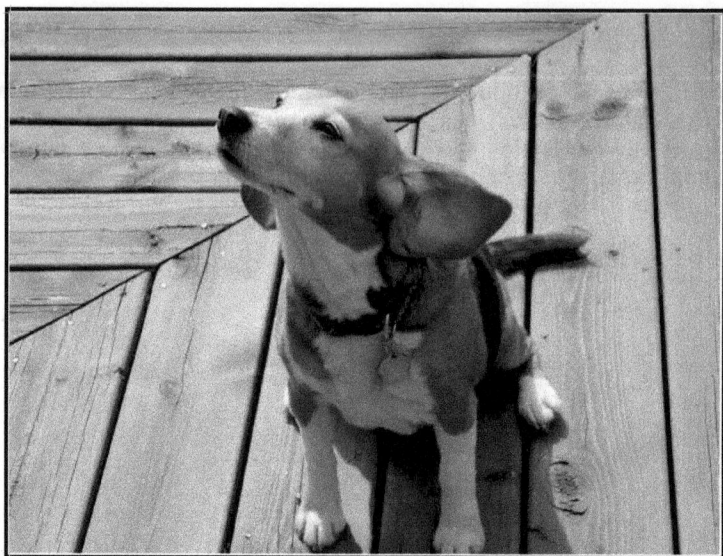

Bess
Photo Courtesy of Sarah Simmons

RESCUED TWICE

Sarah Simmons

Sometimes rescues are a combination of rescuing both dogs and humans. A few years ago, I decided that I wanted another dog as company for my male beagle. We went to a pet adoption at a pet supply store with another dog in mind after having seen a picture of it in the paper. But all it took was to see a darling female beagle rear up on her foster mom with tail wagging and grin on her face, and I was hooked. We set in motion the paperwork to adopt Bess, as she was called, and before long, we were proud to call her our very own.

Bess attached herself to me almost as soon as she came into our house. She was a very needy dog, wanting constant assurance that she was loved and wanted, and did everything she could to please us. She was incredibly sweet, and for a beagle had the thickest, softest fur. Often I would spend time just running my hands through her fur and marveling at how good it felt under my fingers.

But as sweet as Bess was, she didn't come without problems. She had severe separation anxiety. To try and help, we crated her for security. She chewed through the heavy-duty plastic on one, and broke through the bars of the metal cages twice.

We kept her.

Bess had been a street dog for a while, and because food had been scarce for her she'd learned that every meal was to be eaten in a hurry. She managed to somehow get up on the high kitchen counters and eat whatever we left there. She learned how to work the cupboard doors in the pantry where food was stored, and gorge on whatever she found.

We kept her.

She somehow managed to scatter trash from the kitchen wastebasket all over the floor, and once got in my craft box, which held a multitude of craft items including more than a thousand beads, papers, napkins, and various other things. It took me well over an hour to clean up that mess.

We kept her.

We kept her because we loved her beyond all reason, which of course is not a unique trait in dog lovers. I sensed her frantic desire to be loved, even when she was doing unlovable things in our house. I cried for almost an hour when I thought she'd somehow managed to get out of our fenced-in backyard, and I stumbled around in the dark one snowy night with a flashlight to search for her, sure I would never see my beloved dog again. The whole time, she'd been quietly munching on leftover beef juice that my husband had put between our privacy fence and the chain-link fence. Hidden from view from all of us, she was happily wondering what the fuss was when she came out of her hiding spot, licking her chops.

Bess was with me when I lost both my parents, letting me cry in her soft fur, snuggling as close to me as she could because she knew how sad I was. I sat with Bess when we discovered she had a tumor that had to be removed, and again cried in her fur the day she had surgery.

I also cried into her fur for the last time when her kidneys started failing and she had a seizure. I held her close, whispering into her ear that I would see her later, as she left me for a world where she wouldn't be in pain anymore and could eat as much beef juice as she wanted.

I thought I would never love another dog like I had loved my Bess.

It was true.

But I would love another dog who came into my life two months later by way of the humane society, and I loved her just as fiercely as I had loved Bess.

Cassie is a Lab/hound mix who is big, hyper, pulls heavily on the leash and eats a lot. She even gets in the trash sometimes. But she is sweet, plops on our laps because she's still under the impression that she is small, and leans against us for hugs. She puts a paw on us to remind us that she's here, and often lies beside me on the bed while I read. My hands will stroke her fur, and it's at those times when I realize that not only do we rescue dogs who need us, but the dogs rescue us as well.

There is more to **Sarah Simmons** than her love of animals. She graduated with honors from the University of Akron in Ohio with a degree in Elementary Education, and to this day feels there is no greater resource across the country than youth. She is mother to two school-aged children who are active in band, choir, and softball. There is rarely any peace in her home with four dogs, four cats, and two rabbits. Of all the animals in her home, nine are rescues. One of her dreams in life that Sarah hopes to fulfill at some point is to open an animal sanctuary. Until that time comes, she'll give homes to as many animals in need as possible, and, as always, wishing she could do more.

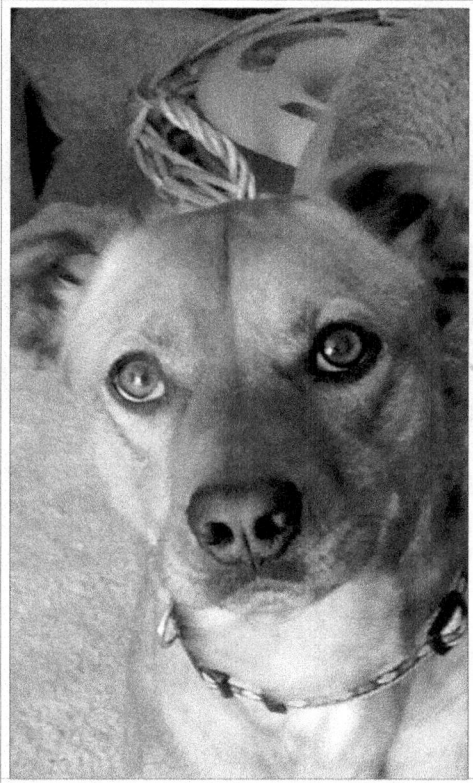

Cassie
Photo Courtesy of Sarah Simmons

Michelle & Topper
Photo Courtesy of Michelle Kuemper

HE RESCUED ME

Michelle Kuemper

Back in the day I always wanted a Husky, so for my birthday in 1996 I received a card from my then-boyfriend, with a picture of a Husky and a note stating I would get my present in the spring.

In the meantime, a friend's mom's Husky had eleven puppies. I had to see them, and I fell in love the fattest, roly-poliest pup, a little male. So I gave a donation of $25 to help cover the first puppy-shots, and was told I could pick the little guy up after Christmas. I couldn't wait.

A few weeks later, when I picked up my puppy, I saw on his veterinarian papers that he'd been born November 11—the very same day as my birthday. I knew this meant he was truly meant to be mine.

Topper, as I named him, was with me through thick and thin, breakups and moves.

He was even stolen once. We were back home at Grandma Pat's, and Topper would get off the leash a lot. When he was

43

off the leash, he would run. He'd been gone for about a day when my Uncle Michael saw Topper at a neighbor's place, and said, "That's Michelle's dog." The neighbor said, "Well, she doesn't seem to want him." Michael didn't argue. He just brought Topper home to me.

Another time Topper went missing in a blizzard, only to be found three days later and thirty miles away. It's in a Husky's nature to run, and since we'd only been in our place for about six months I figured he'd gone in the wrong direction in the blizzard and didn't know his way home yet. He just thought it was fun to go. Typical Husky.

But no matter what happened, Topper always came back to me.

He went everywhere with me. If my pickup left the yard, it was guaranteed Topper would be sitting in the passenger seat. As I drove down the highway, people we met along the way would know it was me when they saw Topper's head hanging out the window.

My Topper dog, from roly-poly puppy to adventurous friend, gave me fourteen years of pure love and happiness.

Then one night I came home after work and found him in the kennel with the two other pupsters, unable to move. He'd had a stroke, which left him paralyzed. I called the vet, who said it was probably time, but as long as Topper was drinking and eating the vet said to wait until Monday so he wouldn't have to charge me for an emergency visit to put Topper to sleep.

For three days I didn't leave my guy's side. Come Monday morning, we made the long trip to the vet to say goodbye. I held his paw as Topper took his last breath. I will forever remember the expression of love and understanding in his eyes.

My home seemed so empty without him. I had Tovey and Tucker at the time and they made me feel better, but those rides in the pickup just weren't the same without Topper hanging his head out the side window.

A year later I went to a gypsy for a life reading. During the reading she abruptly stopped. She said she wasn't afraid, but was a little uneasy about the dog that was sitting next to me. She described my Topper-dog to a T. She told me about the pickup truck that he rode in, the farm, the last day at the vet, and how he hadn't been ready to leave me that day. She couldn't have known any of these details.

I'm at ease now, knowing that Topper is always at my side. That he will always and forever be with me, in memory and with his spirit.

After that visit to the gypsy I got a tattoo. It runs up my side, showing Topper with angel wings, and his paw-prints leading up to my heart. And even now, from time to time I will catch a glimpse of something, maybe a fluff of his fur when I'm feeling sad. Sometimes I'll ask my other pups if they see Topper. Inevitably, they look right at Topper's urn and give small wags of their tails. It truly warms my heart.

And in memory of my old friend I now make and sell homemade dog treats, known as Topper's Treats, creating each batch with the love he shared with me. I miss him every day, but am thankful he was a part of my life.

Michelle Kuemper has loved animals all her life. She has horses and dogs. She does rodeos, trail rides, anything possible with her horses, and with her dogs she runs various "5 K9" marathons with donations going to different animal shelters and programs. Her critters are like her children; she will go without things before they do. They are truly a blessing to have and she's very thankful they have their fur-ever home with her.

Topper
Photo Courtesy of Michelle Kuemper

Emily & Charlotte
Photo Courtesy of Mary Ellen Trombley

ADOPTION DAY

Mary Ellen Trombley

My sister had asked me to stop at PetSmart and pick up some of the special dog food she gives to her two shelties. My three children were with me, shopping for school clothes and we were all exhausted, but I'd agreed to pick up the dog food. What I didn't know was that it was "Adoption Day" at PetSmart.

The moment we walked through the front doors, my kids bolted toward the center of the store, where several penned areas had been set up. Frank, Curtis and Patty were no longer exhausted. They'd been infused with new energy, moving from pen to pen, petting dogs of all sizes and breeds.

One of the pens held half a dozen roly-poly puppies, all with long, black and white fur. Another contained two mid-sized wire-haired terriers. Others were occupied by poodles, Chihuahuas, spaniels—nearly every type of dog you could imagine. The puppies yipped and vied for attention, while calmer dogs just watched the activity around them. Of course my kids were attracted to the puppies. Curtis had already picked one up and sat on the floor with it in his lap. Frank and Patty sat down next to him.

"No, absolutely not," I said. I'd grabbed the dog food my sister needed and I headed for the cash register. "Come on, we need to get home."

I paid for the dog food, carried it out to the car and put the bag in the back seat. Then I went back into PetSmart to face what I knew was going to be a battle. The kids had been asking for a pet for over a year, ever since our sixteen-year-old cat, Muffin, had succumbed to feline leukemia. I'd put them off with the excuse that it was too soon to replace Muffin, but as time went on that excuse held less and less validity. What I didn't tell them was that I found it a relief to no longer have to clean a litter box or vacuum up pet hair on a daily basis. I'd loved Muffin, but I had my hands full keeping up with three children and a husband whose job kept him away from home three weeks out of four.

I found them still with the puppies, in conversation with a representative of the local pet shelter. She was telling them that the puppies were border collies.

"Kids..." I said weakly. I felt my resolve deteriorating.

"Border collies are very high energy," woman from the shelter said. "We try to place them with people who have plenty of land for them to run. Unless you live on an acreage or have a very big back yard, that puppy will grow up to be more dog than you can handle."

I saw their disappointment. Patty, the youngest, looked especially heartbroken.

"Let's look at some of the others," I heard myself saying.

Eventually we found ourselves at the pen with two dogs in it. They were fox terriers, the lady from the shelter told us, and went on to explain the dogs' background. Emily and Charlotte were from the same litter, now about four years old. Their owners had suffered a devastating loss when their house burned down, and had surrendered the dogs to the shelter, asking only that they be placed together, if possible.

I didn't want two dogs. I didn't want *one* dog. But who could resist those big, imploring eyes...both human and canine?

So we went home with Emily and Charlotte, and it didn't take long before I was wondering how our family ever got along without them. They taught the kids responsibility, kept us entertained for hours with their antics, and because they weren't puppies we didn't have to go through the ordeal of house training them. I'm back to vacuuming up pet hair every day, but so what? I figure it's a small price to pay for the joy they've brought to our lives.

Mary Ellen Trombley is a busy administrative assistant at a large, hectic medical office who has found her creative outlet in writing. Currently working on several short stories and a collection of poetry, she often sits at her computer with either Emily or Charlotte curled up at her feet.

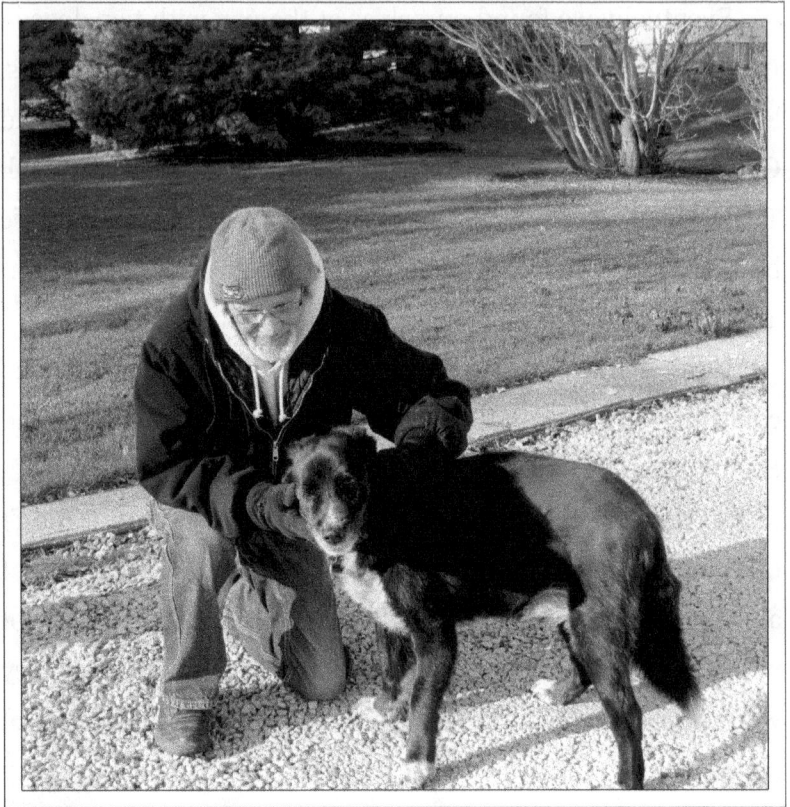

Bill & Jake
Photo Courtesy of Carolyn Rohrbaugh

JAKE, A REASON TO LIVE

Carolyn Rohrbaugh

Bill has always loved animals. Purring cats were stroked as they snuggled beside him on the couch, and dogs always have a special place in his heart.

Throughout his life, pets came and went, always causing a tear to stream down his cheek at another loss. As his wife, I cried with him over the loss of many pets. We buried them all under the weeping mulberry tree in our yard. It seemed like a fitting place.

Each time we said, "No more pets. It's too hard to lose them."

Early one Sunday in January of 2006, our daughter, Traci, called to ask if I would like to go shopping with her, and I gladly accepted. My daughter, daughter-in-law Jonna, two granddaughters, Jaymee and Daneille, and I set off for the one-hour drive in a small, compact car. We were a little cramped, but we barely noticed.

As we stepped into the mall in Sioux City we noticed a crowd gathering around for an event in the center. The Humane Society was there with dogs, cats, and rabbits. Jaymee and Daneille ran straight to a black Lab mix with a fluffy tail that curved over his back. I had to admit, he was handsome.

"Please adopt him, Grandma," they begged. "You know Grandpa Bill will love him."

"No," I told them, "we don't want any more pets."

But each time we walked past him the girls begged me to adopt that dog.

One of the Humane Society workers said, "He's about four years old, and most people don't want an older dog, they want puppies. He's been with us over three months, and we won't be able to keep him much longer."

The granddaughters understood the worker's meaning. They continued to beg and I continued to say, "No."

They finally gave up on me and called Grandpa Bill, telling him the dog was old and would soon be put to sleep.

Grandpa Bill said, "Bring him home, he can be an old dog living with two old people. He'll fit in perfectly."

The five of us climbed back into the small car with all of our packages shoved anyplace we could get them, along with a fifty-pound bag of dog food, and a big black dog on my lap for the hour ride home. He sat there proud and happy. He knew he had been rescued.

We named him Jake, and he is a constant reminder of all the animals who have been rescued and loved.

The lazy life of being an indoor dog, and Bill's love of feeding Jake treats and table scraps, added thirty pounds in four years.

Then the day came that chest pains sent Bill to the emergency room. We suspected a heart attack, but the diagnosis was lung cancer. The removal of a lung and chemotherapy meant that Bill and Jake spent a lot of time lying around.

We soon realized that Bill wasn't the only one with health problems. Jake was also sick, with a diagnosis was diabetes.

Doc Stewart said, "He will need two shots a day and should lose the thirty pounds."

We made a feeble attempt to feed Jake less, but he didn't lose weight and the diabetes wasn't under control.

Then Doc Stewart said, "He won't live long if he doesn't lose that weight."

That was all we needed to hear. I began cooking broccoli, cauliflower, carrots, celery, and hamburger for Jake. We have been feeding him one cup of the vegetable-hamburger mix and two cups of dry dog food twice a day with an insulin shot each time. He doesn't mind the shot and loves the vegetables. We walk him twice a day, and as a result Jake has lost the thirty pounds. And luckily, Bill was pronounced cancer free.

On January 21, 2015, we celebrated nine years with Jake. Four years ago he began losing his eyesight and is now blind, but it hasn't slowed him down. He's about thirteen years old and does very well for an old, diabetic, blind dog. We are thankful for each day with the dog whose life we saved.

Maybe I should say, whose life our granddaughters saved.

He has given us both a reason to live.

Nine years have passed since Jake came into our lives. Bill loved Jake more than anything and enjoyed every day with his gentle friend, who returned his love in every way. In April 2015, Bill's cancer returned and on July 29, 2015 Jake, our family and I lost, Bill, the love of our lives. Jake is failing and spends his days lying beside Bill's empty bed. I dedicate this story to Bill and Jake, two gentle and loving souls.
Carolyn Rohrbaugh

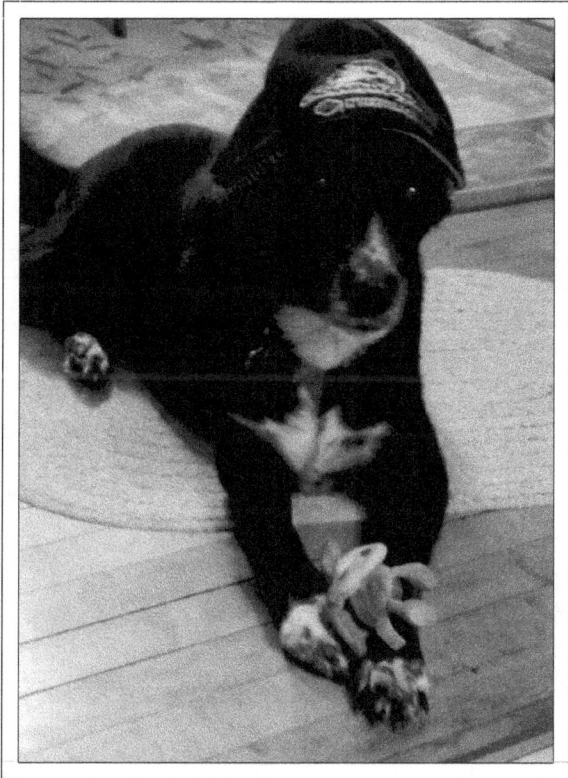

Jake
Photo Courtesy of Carolyn Rohrbaugh

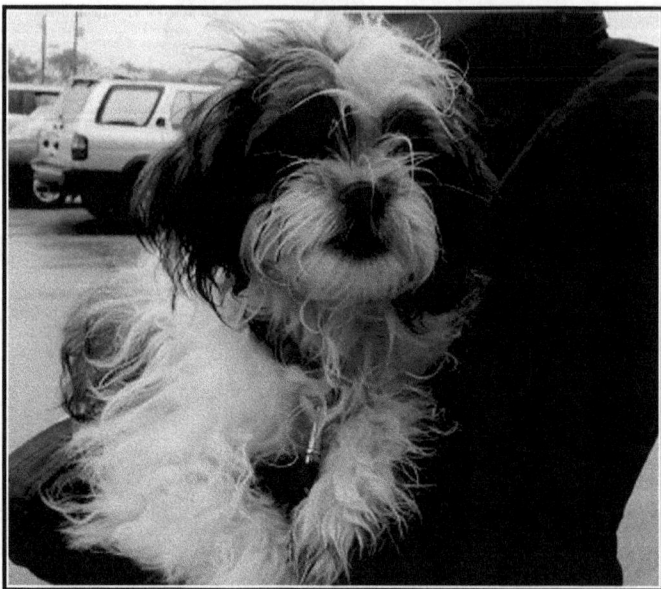

Baby Joey
Photo Courtesy of Phillip M. Ritenour

BABY JOEY COMES HOME

Phillip M. Ritenour

When our family lost our yellow Lab to a sudden illness, we thought we wouldn't get another dog. It had been too painful to say goodbye to Buttercup. But within about six months we could tell the kids wanted a pet. Sarah and I talked about it, then we called the kids in for a family meeting and brought up the subject.

"This family needs a dog," Sarah told them. Tanya and Michael were excited by the idea.

With a little more discussion we agreed we would adopt a shelter dog. We wanted to give a home to a dog that really needed it, and Sarah and I also wanted to teach the kids the value of rescuing an animal. There was a great animal shelter not far from us, so that very next Saturday we all piled into the van and drove there.

"Maybe they'll have another yellow Lab for us," Tanya said hopefully. "A baby, so he can grow up with us."

"That's pretty specific," Sarah said. "But remember, we don't have to bring a dog home today. If we don't find the right one here, we can look at other shelters."

It didn't exactly turn out that way. We walked into the shelter and told the director what we were hoping to find. But while I continued visiting with the director, Sarah and the kids wandered off to look at some dogs. I found all three of them crouched in front of a wire cage. Michael had his fingers poked between the wires, where a shaggy little guy with wide-set eyes and a flat nose was licking them.

He couldn't have been more opposite of what we were looking for.

The description on the door of his cage said his name was Baby Joey. He was a Shih Tzu mix, and labeled as a "senior."

Tanya also reached a hand into the cage and was stroking the dog's head. Despite the attention, his eyes seemed soulfully sad.

The director approached. "Baby Joey is eleven years old," she said. "He came here a month ago when his elderly owner died. The grown children didn't have a place for him, and we promised them we'd do our best to find a home for him. They say he's a very nice dog, but he's been mostly just sad since he got here. I'm sure he's scared and confused by the change in his life. He'd been with one person all of his life."

"This isn't exactly a yellow Lab pup," I pointed out.

My words fell on deaf ears. Sarah turned to me and said, "This is our dog."

I groaned. "Seriously? Can't we at least look around a little more?"

They weren't listening. Sarah, Tanya and Michael had fallen in love. An hour later, after filling out an application and paying the adoption fee, we took Baby Joey home with us. We talked about changing his name. Baby Joey had most likely been appropriate at one time, but it didn't seem so much any more. We didn't want to confuse him any more than necessary, so we just started calling him Joey.

He definitely wasn't a puppy, but as it turned out, that wasn't a bad thing. Joey was well trained, never had an accident in the house and was far past the stage of wanting to chew on everything. He was a cuddler and loved nothing more than to sit on a warm lap to be stroked. When he was in the backyard with the kids he'd gamely chase a ball around for a while, but tired quickly. They didn't mind so much. The love and gratitude he exuded was enough for them.

After about a year with us, Joey developed some health problems. He needed special food and a daily injection of insulin. The kids learned to give him his shots. Sarah began to fret. "What if he dies?" she asked me. "We'll all be heartbroken all over again."

"He will die, eventually," I reminded her.

"I know, but most likely it'll be a lot sooner than we were expecting. What were we thinking, adopting such an old dog?"

"We were thinking we'd found our dog. And we did."

Sarah and I figured the best thing we could do was keep an open discussion going with the kids about the inevitability of losing Joey. They understood more than we had expected them to. We all agreed that we'd done the right thing in making sure Joey's final years were good ones.

As it turned out, our little dog was made of sturdier stuff than we'd realized. Though he is still on a special diet, and gets not only his daily shot but a couple of other medications as well, he is now nearly fifteen and still with us. Tanya is a freshman in high school and Michael is a junior. Every day after school Joey waits for them on the front porch, and when he spots them, all the joyful wiggling he does could almost fool you into thinking he's a puppy after all.

We no longer worry about how much longer we might have with Joey. We're just amazed at how much he has enriched our lives. And now, whenever we hear our friends talking about adopting a pet, we encourage them to consider the older ones. What they might lack in energy, they make up for with an endless supply of love.

Phillip M. Ritenour and his family are happy to report that Baby Joey, now sixteen years old, is still with them and still doing well. They count every day with the little Shih Tzu as a gift, not only because he brings joy to their lives, but because he taught them that love has no age and kindness knows no boundaries.

The average dog is a nicer person than the average person."~ *Andy Rooney*

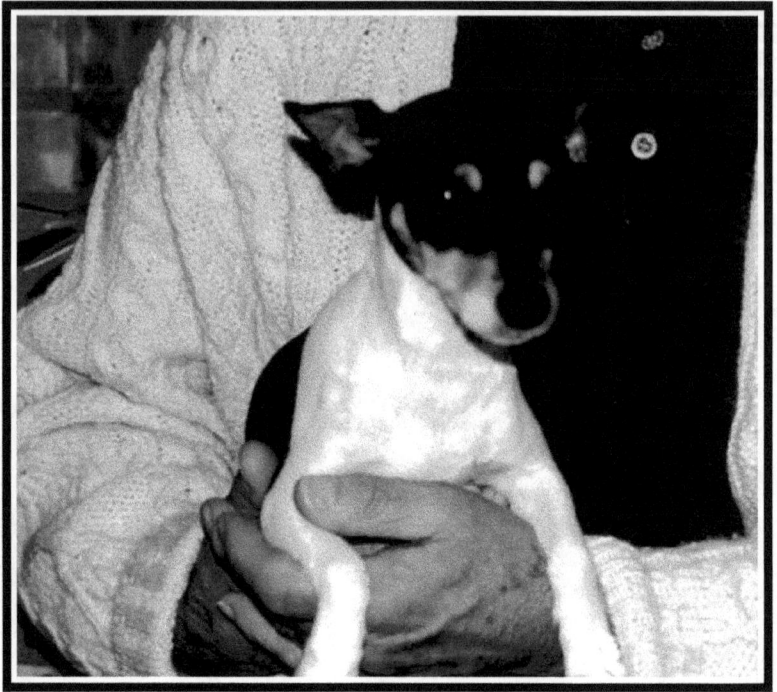

Emilie
Photo Courtesy of Susan Dunn Schmid

EMILIE'S REVENGE

Susan Dunn Schmid

Mrs. Schneider and her herd of goats are our backyard neighbors. Along with the goats and their kids lives a black and white rat terrier who competes with the goats for the fruit and vegetable scraps we take daily to our compost pile. Over time, I took a liking to that dog's endearing temperament and decided, if given opportunity, we'd adopt one like him.

That opportunity didn't come about, but as destiny would have it, we learned early in 2001 that the runt of a litter in Austin was in need of a home. We drove down to claim her. Little Miss Emilie was timid, reserved and so petite that she rode home in my husband, Max's, coat pocket. She stole our hearts with her sweet innocence and settled nicely into our home.

Emilie's main duty each day was to get along with our resident miniature schnauzer, Grethel, who never met a dog she liked. To Grethel, Emilie was a foster child who needed close supervision, and when she'd tire of Emilie's youthful shenanigans, she'd chase Emilie into her miniature dog carrier that we called *The Box.*

It wasn't long after Emilie joined our ranks that I noticed her coat shed little black and white hairs. This wouldn't do on carpeting, so a family rule was established that Miss Emilie was not permitted into the carpeted rooms. To her credit, Emilie quickly learned her boundaries. And Grethel, who didn't shed and had free rein, used Emilie's territorial constraints for additional policing.

Several years of domestic bliss passed before it was time to replace worn carpets. Furniture was moved out and carpet layers moved in to pull up the old and measure, cut and install the new. Strangers always upset our dogs, so we confined them to the family room and kitchen. The workers had begun their day early, so by 3:00 PM they'd wrapped up, and the last van left our driveway. Max, Grethel and I walked around the living room, bedrooms and office with great satisfaction, admiring the fresh, updated look of our home. Emilie stood on the edge of the carpet wagging her stub tail in communal approval.

With this big job done, Max and I decided to celebrate with a drive to nearby Salado for dinner and a little shopping. Grethel loved car rides, but Emilie found them stressful and she'd whine incessantly. Since we hoped for a relaxing outing, we decided to take Grethel and leave Emilie at home to recover from the day's disruptions and anxieties.

Before leaving, I headed to our back bedroom to change clothing. On my return to the kitchen, I noticed a pile of something near the family room door on the newly-laid carpet. As I zeroed in, there was no mistaking it—dog puke! Since Grethel had been outside with Max, the perpetrator of the crime was apparent. I couldn't believe that Emilie had not only stepped onto the forbidden carpet, but threw up on it! Her little head hung in disgrace when I questioned her.

I cleaned the mess and closed the sliding door between the living and family rooms to ensure the offense would not be repeated. As I headed for the garage, I said a quick goodbye to Emilie and glanced into the carpeted office thinking the room should be safe.

The charms of Salado were just what Max and I needed and we returned in a few hours' time refreshed. We entered the kitchen, laid our purchases on the counter, and I headed for the office while Max prepared Emilie's dinner. As I approached, my eyes zeroed in on dark spots on the floor. Entering, I found a large area of the freshly-laid carpet had been soiled and tracked in with feces. My eyes then traced dog-poop paw prints along the full seat-length of our cotton sofa and onto the window sill ledge where a water-filled vase of flowers had been knocked down. The carpet and sofa arm were drenched, and flowers were strewn everywhere. I let out a wail and Max came running. When he grasped the situation, he cried, "Susan, why didn't you shut the office door before we left?!"

While he mercifully commenced clean-up operations, I ran to our computer to send an ardent message of exasperation to my dog-loving sister, Debbie. In it, I poured out details of Miss Emilie's rancorous antics of the day. Here is the response I received:

> *I'm sure you're mistaken about Emilie being responsible for the unpleasantness that took place in your office while you were off having a good time with that OTHER dog. There must be another explanation. . ."*

Little Miss Emilie was a bright, clever character who, despite her petite size and occasional antics, gave us enormous joy. She wasn't with us for many years, succumbing to cancer in 2009, but she lives on in loving familial memory, having left a lasting legacy of her sweet and winsome spirit.

Susan Dunn Schmid is at home in central Texas, where she enjoys retirement with husband, Max, and dog, Heidi. She is proud to be the mother of four children and grandmother to eight grandsons—all of whom are five years or younger! Susan grew up on farms in northwest Iowa where she learned to love and appreciate the beauty and bounty of the earth—and a legion of farm animals that included dozens of beloved cats and dogs. Her heart's desire is to restore life to these simpler times and to be a blessing to her flourishing family.

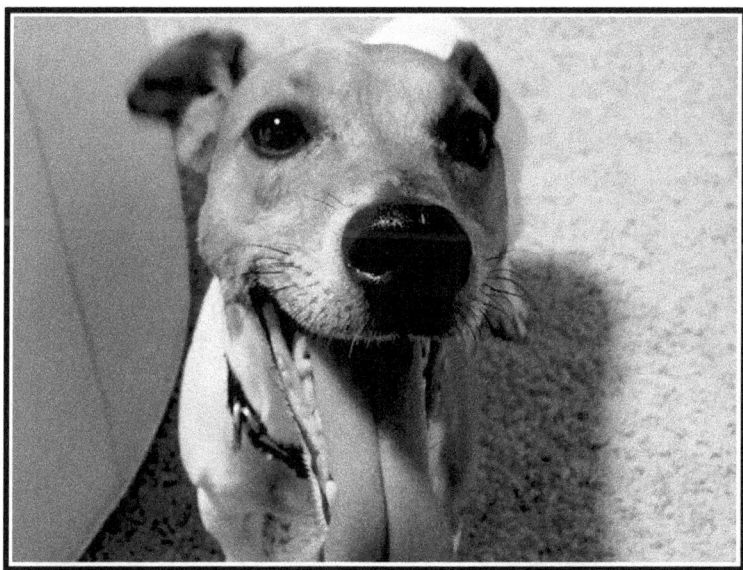

Ike
Photo Courtesy of Stephanie O'Brien

Boomer
Photo Courtesy of Stephanie O'Brien

GORDY AND THE SQUIRRELS

Gray DeMotta

Gordy was found tied to a radiator in an abandoned house. His owners had moved away and left him there with only a bowl of water and a collar that was too small for his neck. When concerned neighbors called the Humane Society, investigators went to the house to find the malnourished Rottweiler.

I decided to adopt him after reading his story on the Humane Society's website. I was alone, and needed a companion. My wife had died several months before, our kids were grown and scattered to the far corners of the county. I liked to visit them, but most of the time I rattled around in that big empty house, feeling the loneliness grow day by day. A dog, I decided, was what I needed. Something small enough that the grandkids wouldn't be frightened by it, but big enough that I could take it for some long, brisk walks.

After seeing the dog's photo online, I decided to go take a look. It was a four-hour drive to the shelter where he was being housed, but I made the trip after first calling to be sure he was still available. He was.

Though the dog was still a little thin, I was told he was eating well and was putting on weight. He'd been neutered, and given all of his shots. He was approximately two years old and on the small side for his breed. Because there had been no identifying tags on his collar, the staff had named him. They called him Gordy.

"Hi, Gordy," I said when they brought him to me on a leash. With the usual black and tan Rottweiler markings, he seemed to be smiling, and his tail wagged as though he knew he needed to as charming as possible.

But I worried. I'd been captivated by this dog's story, but Rottweilers, like pit bulls, were considered a "bully breed." What if he was aggressive? I had grandchildren to think about. I told the shelter workers about my concerns. They questioned me closely about my grandchildren's ages and the time I could devote to proper training of any dog I took in. They also told me that Gordy had been with them for a couple of months and seemed to have an exceptionally sweet nature. He had been fostered by a family with children, and was gentle at all times.

In the end, I couldn't turn away from this dog. It seemed he needed me as much as I needed him. I stayed in town overnight so I could have several visits with Gordy before making a final decision. When I left town the following morning, he was riding shotgun in the front seat of my pickup, still grinning, his head hanging out the window.

I continued to call him Gordy—he responded well to it—and bought him a proper collar and tags with his name, as well as my name and phone number on it. Gordy and I had a full two months together before we would go to visit family. I decided to put the time to good use with some serious socializing. I walked him at least three times a day, stopping to visit with anyone who showed a willingness to do so. I took him to the dog park, and watched closely as he interacted with the other pets there. There seemed to be no mean side to this dog.

The clincher, however, was the squirrels. My big back yard had plenty of trees, and trees mean squirrels. It was spring, and they chattered as they leapt from tree branch to tree branch. The first time Gordy spotted them he had bounded across the backyard in joy, stopping just beneath a tree to stare up into the leaves, that perpetual smile of his widening. He didn't bark at them, which surprised me. He just watched.

"Be careful, squirrels," I whispered as I watched from the back porch. "He's just waiting for you to put your guard down."

That didn't seem to be the case. Gordy loved to run from one tree to the next, his eyes aimed upward at the squirrels, but he looked for all the world like he was hoping they'd come down to play. Then, one afternoon, I looked out and saw

Gordy not looking up into the trees, but instead nosing something on the ground beneath one of them.

Uh, oh, I thought, and headed out there. A baby squirrel had fallen from the nest. It was stunned, but I hoped not seriously hurt. Its light weight, combined with a layer of last fall's leaves, had cushioned the fall. Gordy had nudged at it with his nose, but had done the baby no harm. A couple of squirrels high above scolded us, chattering noisily. Squirrel nests are usually much higher in the trees than birds' nests, but they are larger and easier to spot. The one I saw was at least twenty feet up. I was sure I'd be able to reach it with my best extension ladder.

After putting on some gloves, I placed the squirrel in a dishtowel, the corners of which I tied in a knot behind my neck, so as to have as little contact with it as possible. I hoped the parents would accept it back in the nest. Gordy kept poking his nose at the towel, and I kept pushing him away. I set the extension ladder against the tree, and began to climb, being careful not to bump the dishtowel against the rungs. From far below, Gordy watched. From nearby branches, adult squirrels continued to reproach.

When I was just below the nest, I reached into the pouch with a gloved hand and retrieved the baby squirrel. Then I lifted it above my head and put it in the nest. I wasn't high enough to see inside, and I didn't want to. They were wild animals and needed to stay that way. I could only hope the parents would not reject this young one.

Once I'd climbed back down and put the ladder away, I went back to Gordy and praised him for being a good dog. I also let him sniff the towel, so he would know the squirrel was gone. He grinned at me.

Much of my concerns about Gordy had been relieved. A week later, we drove to visit my son, Scott, and Charlie, my eight-year-old grandson. I had told them about Gordy's background. Scott and I stayed close, keeping an eye on Charlie and Gordy, but they hit it off right away. They wrestled on the floor, Gordy rolling over on his back in submission, allowing Charlie to climb on him until they were both exhausted and fell asleep together on the carpet.

When we got ready to head back home the next day, Charlie stayed at the pickup window, petting Gordy, telling him to come back soon. Gordy looked at me as though asking for confirmation. I assured them both that, yes, we would be back.

And we were, many times. Gordy and I also went to visit my other grandkids. They all loved him, and he loved them in return. And, to a one, they loved hearing the story of the baby squirrel. Instead of giving me credit for climbing twenty feet up on a ladder, they preferred to think Gordy had single-handedly rescued the fallen squirrel by bringing it to my attention.

What the heck, I thought. Gordy had saved me from a life of loneliness, so maybe he was the hero they credited him to be, after all.

Gordy the Rottweiler proved to be so good with children that **Gray DeMotta** began taking him to schools, to educate others on the breed, and to nursing homes, where he is especially gentle with the elderly. Though now eight years old and showing some silver around the nose, Gordy continues to be a happy and energetic dog that still enjoys watching squirrels.

Boomer, Ike, & Delta
Photo Courtesy of Stephanie O'Brien

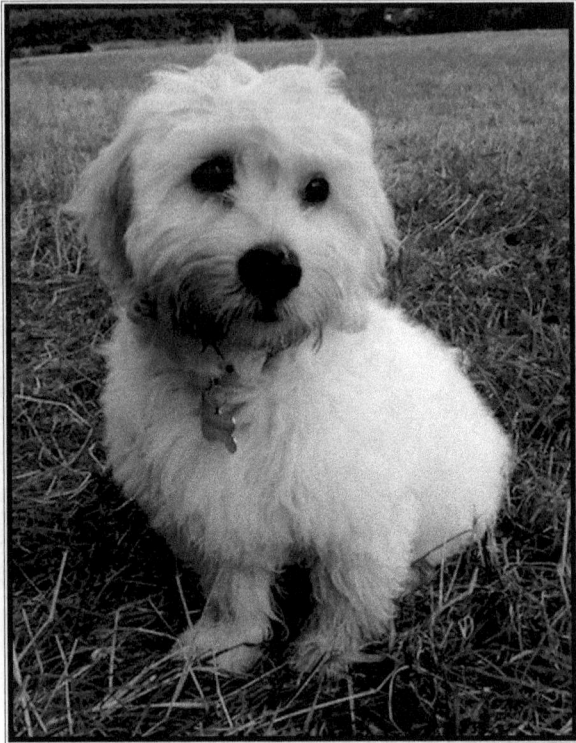

Trixie
Photo Courtesy of Josie Rivara

ON A LONELY ROAD

Josie Rivara

Trixie with me for only two years, but we came together at a time when we both needed someone, and they were two very good years.

Let me back up a bit. I was divorced, had been laid off from my job of eight years, and was worried that my savings would be gobbled up before I could find something else. My adult son lived nearly a thousand miles away. He was not yet married, I had no grandchildren, and my parents were gone. As I drove home on a very dark, rainy night, I was so deep in thought about my troubles that I took a wrong turn and found myself on an unfamiliar gravel road.

Then I saw it. Running along the side of the road, was a dog. I slowed the car, thinking it had to belong to one of the farmhouses nearby. But there were no farmhouses here. Just a long, empty stretch of gravel. As I pulled alongside the still-running dog, I saw that it was dirty and thin, and seemed frightened by the approach of my car.

I passed it, looking in my rearview mirror. The dog continued to run, but I thought it looked tired, so I stopped the car in the middle of the road. Why not? I hadn't seen another vehicle in miles. When I got out of the car, the dog stopped. What was I doing? It was either a stray, or had simply wandered a little far from home and would find its way back. Either way, it wasn't my business. And right now I was having enough trouble taking care of myself.

But I couldn't leave. Something about it touched me. The dog seemed as lost as I felt. I crouched down, snapped my fingers and said, "C'mere, fella."

The dog approached cautiously, tail down. It was medium-sized, with fur that might have been white, once cleaned, and I could see hip bones jutting through the fur.

"Come on, it's okay," I said, softer this time, making my voice high, as though talking to a child.

The dog responded to this. The tail, still down, wagged a little, and came close enough for me to touch it. The rain continued to fall, but at that moment I don't think either of us noticed. We were looking into each other's eyes. I saw infinite sadness in there, and suspected the dog saw the same in mine.

So I took her home. Yeah, the "fella" turned out to be a she, and I started calling her Trixie for no other reason than after I gave her a bath and her coat appeared white and silky, she seemed like a Trixie to me. She ate like she hadn't had anything in weeks, and maybe she hadn't.

I took her to the vet. I really couldn't afford it, but once I'd taken her in I knew she was my responsibility. The vet told me she looked like she'd been neglected for a long time. She had old scars under the fur. She had heartworm. I left with Trixie an hour later and $400 poorer, with medication and instructions on how to administer it. I almost wondered what I'd gotten myself into. Almost.

Trixie hung her head out of the car window as we drove home, ears flapping behind her. Just watching this, and the joy it obviously gave her, was enough to dispel my concerns. That night, even though I'd made up a bed of old blankets in the kitchen for Trixie, she tiptoed into my bedroom and settled on the carpet next to my bed. I looked down at her. She looked up at me.

"Okay, come on up," I said.

She bounded up on the bed so quickly that I knew she'd been waiting for those words. She slept curled up beside me, and I slept better than I had in months.

With this new responsibility, I knew I could no longer afford to wallow in my own misery. I continued my job search, but this time, when I was offered something I previously would have considered beneath me, I accepted. I was one of many administrative assistants in a large insurance office. At first my duties were not much more than filing and answering the phones. Yet each day, when I came home frustrated by being told what to do by women twenty years younger than I was, Trixie greeted me happily, and my burdens disappeared.

Still, she was sometimes fearful. If I reached out to pet her too quickly, she would flinch. I talked to her in a soft voice, telling her I didn't know what had happened to her before, but that I would never mistreat her or desert her. She was safe with me.

Trixie thrived, putting on weight. The heartworm treatments were a success, and her coat glowed with health. Her nervousness disappeared as she realized she could trust me.

At my job, I put aside my attitude and found that the people I worked with were really a pretty good bunch, and I began to receive invitations to lunch. I made friends. My financial situation was no longer so dire, and every night Trixie was a warm, comforting presence.

Then, about a year and a half after she'd come to me, Trixie had a seizure. It passed quickly, but I took her to the vet. He suspected her heart had been weakened by the earlier disease she'd survived. I was given more medications to administer, but the seizures continued, getting worse with each passing week. Though she didn't seem to be in pain, the veterinarian warned me that she would continue to grow weaker.

At work, my friends were sympathetic. The company had paid for me to take several insurance courses, and I had risen from administrative assistant to agent. I was making more money, had more responsibilities, but when I needed to leave to take Trixie to the vet, my bosses were understanding.

Trixie had lost her previous energy, and spent most of her time resting on the carpet, chin on favorite squeaky toy. She could no longer jump up on my bed, but seemed content just to be nearby. Sometimes, when I missed the feel of her next to me too much, I would lift her gently to the bed. At these times she sighed in contentment.

But soon, even that was too much for her. She'd become an invalid. It was time to let her go. Two of my friends from work went with me when I took Trixie for her last visit to the veterinarian. We all sobbed, though I tried to keep up a brave front for Trixie's sake. I was glad I had my friends with me. It would have been too hard to do this alone.

I had Trixie cremated, her ashes put in an urn. That way I could keep her with me. From a rain-swept gravel road, she'd come into my life and made it a better place. I had promised her she would never again be left behind, and it was a promise I would keep.

The title of her story, "On a Lonely Road," comes not only from where **Josie Rivara** found Trixie, but also from the path on which she herself had been. She credits the little dog with saving her life, bringing joy to her world, and putting a smile back on her face.

"Until one has loved an animal, a part of one's soul remains unawakened." ~ *Anatole France*

HIS NAME WAS SWISHER

Arlene Young

I came home from work one afternoon to find my two teen sons, Matthew and Evan, and a friend sitting in the yard on my swing. I knew something was up. And then I saw him—a very young puppy. He had found his forever home. Nothing was going to change that, and I didn't want anything to change it. He started out as Matthew's dog, but Evan was always right there to help.

His name was Swisher and he was the dog that my son, Matthew, had always wanted. A Pit Bull. Not a fierce, scary monster, but a cute bundle of energy who loved everyone and who soon became Matthew's best friend.

He was rescued from a young man who wanted him only as a status symbol and was going to turn him in to the mean, fierce fighting dog that people think of when they hear the words "pit bull." He had kept the puppy in a closet all night and would throw him against the wall in the morning if he'd had an accident overnight. In order to show Matthew and

Evan how tough the puppy was, the man had picked the puppy up by his ears. Of course, Swisher was crying and trying to get away, but the owner held on until Matthew took the puppy away from him. My sons had heard about this puppy and how he was being abused, so they offered the man $50 for him. Since the man had learned he couldn't keep a dog at his apartment, he agreed, and Swisher was rescued.

In spite of the horrible way he'd been treated, Swisher was forgiving. He was happy to be with Matthew and Evan and never seemed to hold a grudge. He was a great ambassador for the breed that everyone thinks of as terrifying and dangerous.

I didn't help with the house training. I wanted my sons to do this and they did a great job. I had to laugh one morning, though, when Matthew told me that house training this puppy was a lot more work than he remembered from the last puppy we'd had. I just looked at him and laughed. "Yes. I imagine this is more work for you. I did it for all the other puppies." Matthew just grinned.

Swisher was all puppy. I lost a dress coat, a pair of shoes and a borrowed book to the teeth of this little critter. He seemed to target my things when I wasn't home.

When Matthew joined the Army, I knew I had to do more to bond with Swisher, so I signed him up for an obedience class. He loved the other people and their puppies. By now Swisher had developed a habit of sitting either on your feet or so close to your leg that he would fall over if you moved. If he wanted to be petted, he would immediately sit on your feet effectively preventing you from ignoring him or being able to walk away. After he received his pat, he would get up and move out of your way. But he did this on his own terms, not because he was asked to sit.

He demonstrated this technique in obedience class. We were to join up with the pair across from us for an exercise. The lady across from me knew mine was a pit bull and made it very clear she thought he should not be in the class. She said he was dangerous and she wouldn't work with me. The instructor of the class said she was free to leave any time, but the pit bull was not leaving. He then asked if someone else would partner with us. A man with a cute little black and white fur ball raised his hand and crossed the room to stand next to us. I was so thankful for his support of my dog.

Our instructor came over and asked me if he could use Swisher for a demonstration. I handed him the leash and crossed my fingers. The instructor walked Swisher to the center of the room and told him to sit, which Swisher immediately did. On the instructor's feet. The instructor just looked down at him with a smile on his face and asked the class if this was the picture of a big, bad pit bull? I heard some chuckles and then the instructor suggested everyone come over to meet Swisher and to bring their dogs.

The instructor went out of his way to show everyone in the class that this was simply a happy dog that loved people and other puppies, as well.

We worked hard to finish the class and graduate. In order to graduate, each dog had to learn to sit, stay and come on command. Swisher had learned the sit command early on, but wouldn't come on command. He just didn't want to come when called. He came to me when he was ready and if there were treats involved. He trained us to carry treats at all times.

Swisher began his life in an abusive home, at the hand of a cruel and heartless owner, but never held his early abuse against us. He gave us the chance to show him what it was like to live in a loving home where he was treasured.

Swisher had a chance to adopt a new friend when I brought another puppy home that I rescued from the local shelter. I was worried there would be trouble and that Swisher would not accept the new puppy, named Morgan. I should have known better. I came home one day to find Matthew, who was home on leave, sitting on the kitchen floor with the new puppy in his lap and Swisher next to him. Matthew had gotten the message to Swisher that this puppy was not a toy and was here to stay.

From that first day, the two dogs were best friends. They ate together, sat on the couch together and tried to cuddle on your lap together.

Not long after Morgan came into the house, Evan moved into his own place, taking Swisher with him. Morgan stopped eating. Swisher also had stopped eating. Evan brought Swisher home for a visit and those two dogs ate every bit of dog food I had. Sometimes Morgan would growl and make

Swisher move away from the food and Swisher always did. I don't think Morgan ever realized he was playing with a dog that most people were afraid of. Morgan just knew Swisher was his buddy.

Swisher lived with us for 13 years. We lost him on New Year's Eve and have missed him every day since. Morgan misses him as well.

Everyone should be as lucky to find such a wonderful dog to rescue. There's never been a day when I've regretted that my sons stepped up and did the right thing for a sweet pup. Swisher gave us his unconditional love and the many memories that we hold close to us.

A native of Wyoming, **Arlene Young** now makes her home in Iowa. This is her first published story. Arlene is a single mother of three amazing grown children and has just become a new grandma for the first time. Aside from creative writing, her other interests include riding and training horses, growing beautiful flower gardens and spending a good amount of time every day with Morgan, her wonder dog.

Buddy & Bonnie
Photo Courtesy of Bonnie Boeck Ewoldt

KONG TIME

Bonnie Boeck Ewoldt

*"The great pleasure of a dog is that you may make a fool
of yourself with him and not only will he not scold you, but
he will make a fool of himself too."* Sam Butler

If someone had told me a couple of months ago that I would
drop everything to dash outside to play a few rounds of
Kong at every opportunity, I would have said they were crazy.
I never dashed outside for anything, nor was I familiar with a
slimy, gravely, mass of rubber affectionately known as Kong.
A black Lab named Buddy changed all that.

Buddy was a rescue dog who came home with us one
January as an 18-month-old pup. His first days with us were a
bit of a trial when we discovered he is a chewer, and not your
typical puppy-type chewer that snatches slippers, gloves, and
stuffed toys. Buddy was a CHEWER on steroids, capable of
destroying anything within reach—boxes of Christmas
decorations, leather boots, wooden chairs, woodwork, tree
branches, and utility cables!

We quickly learned he needed to be confined and carefully watched for our sanity and his own protection.

Buddy is a retriever and a rescue dog that had been shuffled from shelter to shelter. Consequently, he had a high anxiety level combined with an instinctive desire to mouth everything in sight.

We attempted to assuage his chewing fetish by purchasing bags of rawhide bones and similar doggie toys. The rawhide bones are designed to last for days. When Buddy demolished the first one in minutes, it became obvious that we couldn't afford to keep him supplied with fixes for his oral obsession.

About this time, a dog-lover friend suggested we try Kongs, which are hard rubber toys made especially for aggressive chewers like Buddy. I had never heard of them, but was able to find and purchase one online. I was pleasantly surprised, and greatly relieved, to see it was an immediate hit with Buddy. Designed with a hole at the end for stuffing treats and peanut butter inside, the Kong kept him happily chewing away for days.

Two months have passed since Buddy arrived, and he's become acclimated to his new environment.

Puppies are like babies. They explore the world with their mouths. Much of Buddy's chewing was simply his way of learning about his surroundings. Now that he has grown accustomed to being here, the mega-chewing episodes have ceased. The Kong, however, has become his constant companion, not for chewing but for playing. Like a little boy carrying his baseball mitt everywhere, Buddy carries his Kong in his mouth, hoping to find someone with time for a quick game of fetch.

No matter what I am doing when Buddy brings his Kong, I head to the backyard for a couple of tosses. He is a magnificent retriever, able to catch on the fly, on a bounce, out of bushes, or out of low-hanging branches. He can even find his Kong in the dark! Of course, the Kong is not in pristine condition as when it was new. It has transformed into a slobbering mass of hard rubber, covered with dirt, sand, and dead grass. Even so, I don't hesitate to pick it up and throw it whenever he drops it at my feet. I keep my yard gloves in my pocket for those occasions.

Buddy and his Kong have enriched my life. It is true, as Julie Church said of her dog, "I'm joy in a wooly coat, come to dance into your life, to make you laugh!"

Maybe you also have a dog or maybe you have no desire to own a dog. It doesn't matter. What matters is that each of us takes time to do what Buddy taught me—enjoy some Kong Time every day. Kong Time is a spontaneous moment of fun that happens for no reason other than to us smile.

Bonnie Boeck Ewoldt has been a dog lover since her Uncle Paul gave her a puppy named Skippy for her first birthday. Her love of dogs has taken her on many adventures, ranging from breeding purebred Basset Hounds to adopting rescue dogs. Bonnie and her husband, Virgil, live on an acreage in northwest Iowa where Buddy and his feline friend, Sox, rule.

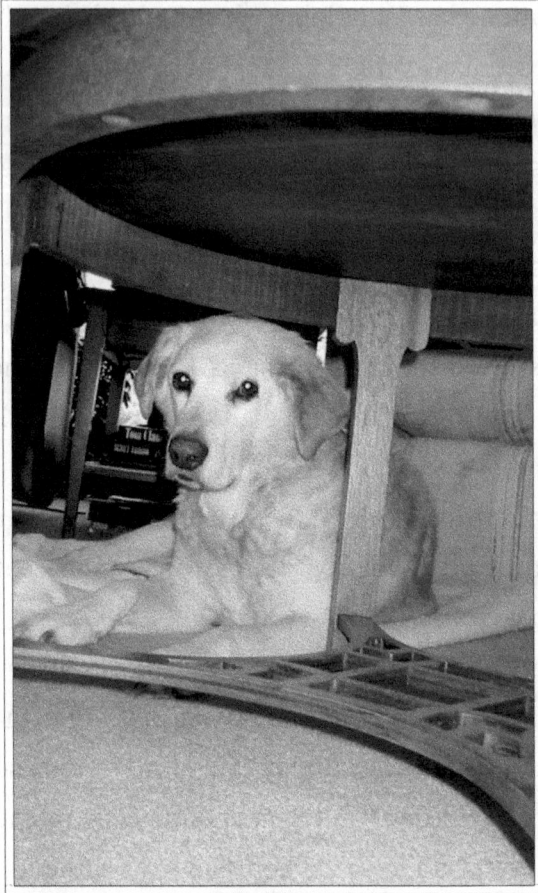

Ginger
Photo Courtesy of R'Becca Groff

THIRD TIME'S A CHARM

R'becca Groff

Somebody's pure bred Husky papa got too friendly with somebody else's Irish setter/Lab-mix mama, producing nine puppies that needed homes.

By the time I saw the ad in the paper and made the call, there were only four left. Three boys and one girl. I knew I wanted a girl and hoped she'd be a good fit for us. Our family had been without a fur buddy for over a year, and my pet-owning instincts had set me to perusing the local newspaper ads the past many weeks.

My husband is a cat person by default, having grown up on a farm where kittens were as abundant as freshly laid eggs. And even though my heart embraces anything with fur and four legs, I always went the dog route for family pets. Every ten years or so our family acquired a new canine member, with these adoptions always occurring while my husband was away on business. He'd fly off to some distant meeting, and *voilà*, when he returned, we had a new family member complete with four feet and wet nose. To date, this phenomenon has rendered three canine children.

Fate smiled on this third occurrence, however. My two young daughters and I took a car ride that day and laid eyes on the runt of the litter, a ginger-colored pup that looked like a purebred Lab. We paid two more visits to her and her mama's owner, a man named Duane, who drove truck for a living while studying with a Franciscan order. The puppy couldn't have had a better caregiver. Being the littlest of the litter, she'd been too weak to suckle on her own, but Duane made sure she got next to her mother, even during the wee hours of the night.

"Take her home," he told us. "Show her to your husband. If he doesn't want her to stay, you can bring her back." He didn't have to say it twice.

My husband arrived home that night to find a quiet, polite nine-pound yellow Lab look-alike waiting for him.

"Ta-daaaaa!" we shouted as he opened the door. "We got you a new dog!"

She crawled between his feet, lay down and went to sleep.

We named her Ginger.

Ginger became a permanent family member. She chewed on sticks, Frisbees and empty milk jugs. She explored our large fenced yard, the little bell on her red collar jingling to let us know where she was.

As she grew, she barked and argued with the neighbor's cats every time they trespassed on her yard. She greeted visitors at the door with curiosity and friendliness, understanding that if we liked them and accepted them in our house, she could too.

Our kids rode the school bus and our youngest daughter always got off one street early cutting through yards and climbing over our back fence to take the shortcut home. Ginger came to expect this. She ran to the back window when she heard the bus roaring past our house. The minute she spied Jen coming, Ginger's tail twitched to a full wag. I'd let her out and she'd take off on a full gallop.

When our kids moved on to high school the bus rides ceased. Still, when the school bus revved around the corner, Ginger would run to that back window waiting and watching. Of course no one came. The first time I witnessed this it broke my heart, but Ginger eventually adjusted, and so did I.

The tennis ball and the Frisbee throws continued as did the long walks and the buddy time watching TV together. Ginger never tired of sharing snack bites from plates, and sitting by the kids through the years as they unwrapped birthday presents and Christmas gifts.

We were going out of town for a weekend and needed to board Ginger, as it was not possible to take her with us. We'd laid out her dishes, pink fleece blanket and toys on the garage floor in preparation for the stay at the kennel.

As my husband busily packed the car, Ginger sat patiently, waiting—obviously sure that it would soon be time for her to take her place in the car for the trip with us. When he opened the driver's door she took her cue, grabbing her pink blanket in her mouth, hopping across his seat and into the passenger side, she looked at him as if to say, "Okay, let's go. I've got what I need." It took some coaxing to persuade her back out of the car that day.

My husband often joked that the dog was glued to my backside. And figuratively speaking, he was absolutely right. Whether I worked in the kitchen, at the computer upstairs, or lounged on the sofa watching television, she remained within tripping range, something I hardly minded. If I was absent from the house for a week now and then, the family told me how she paced the floor at night, searching, ending up alongside my bed, sniffing the covers as if I might finally be found.

But Ginger devoted equal time to my husband's you-know-what as well, especially when she'd see him pulling on work boots in preparation for mowing. If we forgot to let her out she'd pace at the double glass doors, whining and barking until someone set her free.

When she caught up with the John Deere, she'd run alongside, finally content to participate. Even as the arthritis set in and she grew increasingly stiffer, she maintained her tenacity to run the line with her master, coming in the house and collapsing on the cool kitchen floor afterwards, exhausted, but satisfied.

But the signs couldn't be ignored. Ginger began having trouble getting up in time to make it outdoors to do her duties, and late one summer evening she had a seizure. I sat stroking her head and talking to her; her breathing calmed and she went to sleep. And she did wake the next morning.

For the next three days this incredible yellow Lab mix astonished us. She devoured oatmeal and scrambled eggs, eager as a pup, and insisted on being outdoors with us. As I think back on it now, I believe she knew we needed to see her moxie one more time before she left us. Four days after her seizure, and two months past her sixteenth birthday, she decided to go.

Recently, a friend of mine came to visit. She told me she'd put her twenty-year old cat to sleep, and we shared tears over the difficulty of that decision and the pain of losing our beloved pets. And then she said something miraculous to me. "Ginger's still here. I felt her as soon as I walked in."

You're wondering if we've adopted another dog. The answer is no. We rescued a cat this time. I figured it was my husband's turn since I'd always had the dogs. Lexi is buff-colored with white paws and a white tummy—like Ginger was. And she is my shadow—like Ginger was.

Every now and then Lexi turns spooky-acting, going in circles and looking overhead as if she's seeing something we can't. We simply tell her to say, "Hi."

We figure it's Ginger hovering, teasing and tormenting her, and demanding to know why in the heck we brought this cat into her house.

R'becca Groff is a former engineering administrative assistant who enjoys writing from the perspective of her small-town upbringing. She writes a column about local businesses for the *Cedar Rapids Gazette,* and has published in regional, as well as, national anthologies and magazines.

Find her at www.Facebook.com/Rebecca.Groff, or her blog, *http://rebeccasnotepad.wordpress.com.*

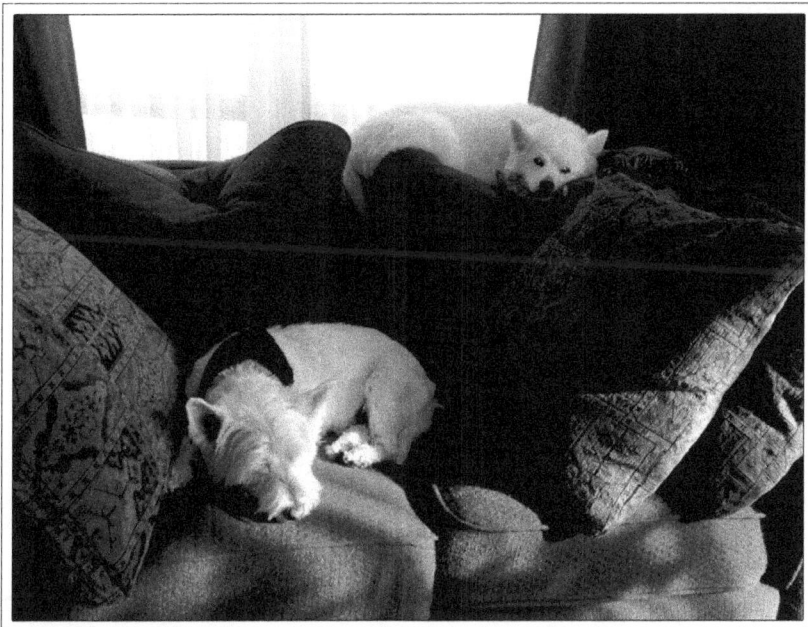

Kirby & Dakota

"Happiness is a warm puppy." ~ *Charles M. Schulz*

JUNIPER'S STORY

Darwin Hagarty

The brown and white dog rested in my arms, her silvered muzzle hanging over my elbow, and I lowered my head to put my mouth close to her ear.

"You're a good girl, Juniper," I whispered. "You're the best dog in the world. I'm so lucky to have you."

Against my other elbow her tail thumped weakly. She agreed with me. And why shouldn't she? I'd been telling her this for the past twelve years.

As an only child, I had always been on the lookout for an excuse to break away from the adults and find more interesting things to do. My parents had divorced and my father was in the service, so I didn't see much of him. Maybe because of that, my mother took me everywhere with her. Whether I wanted to go or not. She dragged me along to visit my many aunts, her sisters, to appointments, and to the old folks' home when she went to visit an elderly neighbor I barely remembered.

It was during one of these Sunday visits when I was ten that I slipped away for a few minutes. I was exploring the grounds behind the building, working my way through a thick hedge of Juniper bushes toward a nearby playground. The bushes were thick and overgrown. They scratched my arms, but I was almost through when I tripped over a cardboard shoebox tucked near the base of a bush. I might have fallen and crushed the shoebox, but instead I came down beside it. With my face in the dirt, the side of the box was near my nose, and I heard a small sound. Like a weak whimper. I reached one hand out to lift the lid and peeked inside.

There were three tiny puppies in there. Two were already dead. The sound I'd heard had come from the one puppy that still clung to life. It was no larger than the palm of my hand, with brown and white fur. I was no expert on dogs, but I'd seen enough of them to know that it was barely a few weeks old.

I lowered the lid and backed out of the bushes. Now what? My mother's visits here usually lasted at least a couple of hours. And I knew the ladies working in the kitchen would give me a snack if I asked.

First I stashed the shoebox in the back seat of our car. Then I ran back inside and made a beeline for the kitchen. There I was given a glass of water and half a sandwich. Roast beef—perfect!

Back to the car, where I gently lifted the surviving puppy from the box and coaxed some water down its throat. I could almost see the little dog's strength returning. Then I tore tiny pieces of beef from the sandwich, but had less luck with the meat. The puppy had tiny sharp teeth, but hadn't yet figured out what do with them.

An hour later my mother came outside to our car and found me sitting in the back seat. "Well, Gladys was chattier than usual today," she said as she slid in behind the steering wheel. She turned and looked at me. "Have you been here all this time?"

"No, I went to the kitchen and got a sandwich," I told her. At my feet the shoebox rested. I prayed the puppy wouldn't make any noise.

"Oh, that's good," Mom said. She seemed preoccupied. A short while later we were home, and she walked into the house without looking back at me. That gave me the chance I needed to smuggle the shoebox into my bedroom.

The dead puppies were still in there, with the live one. I hadn't had the heart to just leave them in the dirt below the Juniper bushes. All three of the puppies had obviously been abandoned to die. I couldn't be a part of that cruelty.

So I wrapped the two dead puppies gently in an old towel from our laundry room. I put the bundle on the floor of my closet, and went to the more urgent matter at hand—the surviving sibling. With a second towel I'd taken, I cleaned the puppy off and gave it more water. I used a pair of flannel pajama bottoms to line the shoebox, then put the puppy back in. It was moving around more now, and beginning to cry for food. Loudly.

It was no longer on the brink of death. It was hungry, and it was letting me know. Even with my bedroom door closed, I worried that my mother would hear it. But she was in the kitchen, and I hoped she would stay there for a while longer.

Somehow I managed to smuggle some food into my bedroom to feed the female pup. Bread softened with milk, cottage cheese, bits of roast chicken—she ate until she had no more room, then fell into a deep, satisfied sleep. Of course I named her Juniper.

After supper, while Mom was on the phone with one of my aunts, I took the towel with the two dead puppies outside. I buried them in a far corner of the backyard, under some rose bushes. As I patted down the dirt with my hand, I whispered, "I'm sorry this happened to you."

Juniper thrived. She figured out her teeth and soon could eat almost anything I brought her. She grew stronger, and started climbing out of the shoebox.

How I managed to keep her secret for a full week is something of a miracle in itself. But finally my mother caught on when she heard a puppy's yip in my room.

"Darwin Harold Hagarty, what do you have in there?" she demanded.

The whole story came out—finding the shoebox, burying the dead puppies, nursing Juniper back from the brink. Mom picked up the chubby, squirming pup and turned her over.

"You've had her in here all this time? Well, you've done a good job of keeping her clean. Is that why you've been doing your own laundry lately?"

"Can I keep her?" I asked. I hated the quiver in my voice but couldn't help it.

With the puppy tucked under her chin, Mom looked at me. For a long, horrible moment I thought she would say no. I'd asked for a puppy on many occasions, and she always said they were too much work, or we didn't have room, or... something.

Then, something amazing happened. Mom said, "Yes. Yes, Darwin, you can keep her. After all you've done to keep her healthy and safe, I think you've earned the privilege."

And so it was that Juniper moved out of my bedroom and became a part of the family. She grew fast, maturing to a mid-size sixteen pounds, a terrier mix with lots of personality who liked to sit on Mom's lap in the evening when we watched TV. She greeted me every day when I got home from school, and during the summers she followed me everywhere. She had her own Christmas stocking that hung beside mine, and she was a in every family photo, head cocked to one side, ears flopping forward.

One day Juniper ran out into the street and was hit by a kid on a motorcycle. I drove the car to the veterinarian's office while Mom held Juniper on her lap, tears in her eyes. The three of us got home hours later, Juniper with a cast on her broken hind leg.

And when I left for college a few years later, of course Juniper stayed with Mom.

Other than the mishap with the motorcycle, Juniper was healthy and active. Until the day when, during a routine visit for her yearly shots, the vet found a lump high on the inside of the leg that had been broken. Sometimes Juniper limped, but we had chalked it up to age, and maybe a little arthritis from the old injury. But it was cancer, and already so advanced that the vet advised against putting her through painful treatments that would most likely do little good.

I'd finished college by that time, and started a new job. As luck would have it, I had moved back home to save money until I could afford my own place, so I was in my old bedroom the night I heard Mom crying softly in her room.

Juniper went downhill quickly, as the vet had predicted. Mom and I took care of her, but all too soon we knew our little dog was in pain, and the time had come. Again I drove to the veterinarian's office, while Mom held Juniper on her lap. In the end, Mom couldn't stay in the room. She just couldn't. But that was okay. It had been just Juniper and me at the beginning, and it seemed fitting that it would be just to the two of us at the end, as well.

I held her and told her what a good dog she was, and she agreed with me.

We buried Juniper in the back yard, under her favorite tree. But it's not an unmarked grave for our girl. On the spot is a stone with her name engraved on it, as befitting a member of the family.

Darwin Hagarty began, with Jupiter, a lifelong dedication to rescuing stray animals. Over the course of the past four decades he has either adopted or found homes for countless dogs, cats, rabbits, a few horses, and even a couple of emus. He has photos of most of them, but, sadly, all photos of Juniper were destroyed in a basement flood a few years after her passing. However, Juniper still is, and will forever remain, fresh in his mind.

Chief
Photo Courtesy of Janet Branson

REMEMBERING CHIEF

Janet Branson

Chief was our youngest son Jeff's dog. He was affectionately called "Chiefy" most of his life. He was part German shepherd, part Rottweiler and almost the sweetest dog I've ever known. Jeff's children were three and almost two when he and his wife Angie brought Chief home from the animal shelter. He was just a puppy and it was love at first sight.

He was wonderful with children, his or anyone else's. Angie baby-sat for a little guy named Jordan for several months. Jordan would climb all over Chief, who would just lie there and let him do it. When Chief was playing with the neighborhood children none of the parents needed to worry about them. No one ever tested his ability to take care of his own. At his maturity he weighed 125 pounds.

One summer afternoon my granddaughter, Mikayla, and I arrived at Jeff and Angie's house and they weren't home yet. Chief met us at the door, and I'm sure I heard him say,

"Howdy folks. Mom and Dad and the kids aren't home but they'll be here soon. Come on in and make yourself comfortable. There is pop in the refrigerator, and snacks, too, I'm sure. I know you're probably tired from your long trip. Go ahead, take a shower, take a nap and refresh yourself if you like. I'll be right here if you need anything."

Jeff worked at the feedlot for his father-in-law, feeding cattle, driving tractor and irrigating. Chief liked nothing better than to go to work with him. He didn't bother the livestock, in fact they intimidated him, but he loved to ride in the truck. He also followed Jeff around and around the field, running beside the tractor until he was tired. Then he'd wait in the shade under the truck.

Chief always got up early and went to work with Jeff. One morning when Angie woke up, Chief was still sleeping and Jeff was gone. She put the dog outside to do his business while she got ready for work. When it was time to leave, she opened the door to let him in but he wasn't there. She called and called, but no Chief. She hopped in the car and finally found him, a half mile away trotting toward the feedlot, going to work.

I'm sure he was thinking, *Oh, Dad isn't going to be happy with me today.*

Angie took him the rest of the way and he was happy to get to work, finally.

He loved to go camping with the family at the lake. One of his favorite games was to fetch a stick or the tennis ball. He would play fetch until everyone else was tired.

We were all lounging on the deck one evening many years ago. Angie was sitting on the porch swing. He crawled from his resting place over to her feet, looking up with big, pleading, teen-age puppy eyes. She totally ignored him. Quietly he eased one foot up onto her lap, then a bit later the other front foot and finally managed to bring his back feet up too. It was like he was thinking if he did this very slowly she wouldn't notice that he was on her lap.

Some time ago he started having problems climbing the steps and all he wanted to do was lie around, which wasn't like him at all. Angie got him some doggie Advil and arthritis meds. He wasn't willing to take either one, no matter how she hid the medicine; he'd feel it in his mouth and spit it out. Finally she hid it in a piece of bologna and he wolfed it down. It worked a miracle for Chiefy. In a few days he was back to his old self and everyone was *so* glad.

Their best friends lived just across the street and through the block. The friends had a lovely little Sheltie who was also Chiefy's best friend. They liked to visit each other two or three times a day. Chief had a doggy door inset in the patio doors and they were free to come and go as they wished. In the mornings he would go outside and make his rounds of the neighborhood, greeting the cows in the pasture next to his house and any neighbors who might be outside. In a while he'd come back home and wait for his doggie friend to come visit. They would lie there on the floor until the friend decided to go home. It was a sad day when the Sheltie was hit by a car and went to his shiny white doghouse in the sky.

A few years ago Chief went with his family to our Branson reunion in Idaho, at Uncle Al and Aunt Barb's place in the woods near a lake. There were a lot of people to play with him and take him for walks. He had so much fun. The plan was that two of our sons and their families were going to go through Yellowstone Park on the way back home. They didn't want to take Chiefy because of the bears and having to leave him in the van for periods of time, so I told them, "He can stay here for a few days and go back with us." Problem solved.

The morning we were to leave he was outside with my husband, who was loading suitcases and things into the van. Chief observed all this and was right on his heels. All the doors were open when Barb came out with an old but clean rug and put it on the back seat for Chief. He hadn't seen that rug before, but as soon as she put it on the seat he jumped in, lay down on that rug and stayed there for the entire trip. We took his water, food dishes and his lead, then climbed in and headed down the road. He was a lovely traveling companion, content to lie there on the seat. We stopped a while later, around lunch time, and opened the door and called him to come out, but he wouldn't move. For that entire nine-hour trip he would not get out of the van until we came to his house. He was taking no chances of being left behind again.

That wonderful dog brought his family so much joy in his lifetime. It was a sad, sad, *sad* day last summer when, at the age of fourteen and a half, he went to his beautiful, shining, sparkling white doghouse in the sky, where he romps the meadows with his long-time Sheltie friend.

Janet Branson lives in Hartley, Iowa, where she started writing only a few years ago, after retiring from an earlier career as a school cook. Her husband is a retired Iowa Baptist pastor. Her other interests include genealogy and antiquing. She has rebuilt and refinished all the furniture that she has in her home. She has even built some of it.

Sonic & Tails
Susan Chappelear

A TALE OF TWO DOGS

Susan Chappelear

I wasn't paying much attention to our "hounds from the pound" when yelps and howls pierced my peaceful morning. Stretched out on the wicker sofa in our sun-filtered screened-in-porch, savoring the last seconds of peace, I exhaled. As I dropped *The Washington Post* and set my mug on the table, coffee splashed over the edges.

Hurrying through the house, I found the dogs, Sonic and Tails, swirled in a wild frenzy in the middle of the family room carpet.

Five years earlier my husband John, and Dayton, our ten-year-old, had discovered Sonic hiding in the back of a kennel at the local animal shelter. He was thin, black and brown with white patches on his chest and paws, and looked a bit like a German shepherd. Like magnets to a needy cause, John and Dayton were drawn to Sonic straightaway.

The woman at the center noticed their interest. "Oh you don't want him. He's not good with kids, climbs fences and he's been returned three times already." She proceeded to share the rest of his unfortunate story, and the deal was sealed. He was coming home with us. We had a tough time at first. It took him a long while to trust us and know that we were his forever home.

More recently we'd brought Tails home. When we first met him his name was Ocho, and he was an adorable ball of black fur. He was busy tolerating another puppy in a shared kennel at the same animal shelter. My son spotted him and it was love at first sight. He was on hold for someone else, but as it turned out the little guy ended up with us.

Dayton renamed him Tails to go with Sonic, after two characters in his prized video game, Sonic the Hedgehog and his sidekick, Tails.

But now, things seemed to be going terribly wrong.

"Sonic, Tails!" I screamed their names and grabbed for the collars. At first I thought Sonic, the five-year-old, 80-pound dog was attacking the puppy, as his teeth appeared to be clamped around the smaller dog's neck.

"What's happening?" Dayton rushed in and threw himself into the mix in a desperate attempt to separate the dogs.

John appeared in the doorway. He paused for a moment, a confused look on his face, and made a dash for our son. He wrenched Dayton from the dogs and deposited him on the nearby sofa. Horror on his face, Dayton slid off the cushion and onto his knees, folded his hands and squeezed his eyes shut.

John reached his arms around the dogs, slowed their frantic thrashing and got a closer look. "It's Sonic's teeth. His incisors are caught in Tails' collar."

They both wore thick leather collars with big buckles. The puppy had grown so quickly that his was too tight. As Sonic shook his head, he tossed Tails back and forth like a rag doll.

Darting to the kitchen, I retrieved my scissors, the kind that can cut a penny in half. "Here, try these." I handed them to John.

No luck. He dropped them on the floor and raced to the garage. He returned with garden shears. The leather twisted between the blades.

I crouched on the floor with the dogs. Tails was being strangled and losing consciousness, his bowels emptied on the floor. My shirt was torn, my arms covered in cuts and scratches; cheeks damp; clothes and carpet smelled of blood and feces.

Dayton doubled over on the floor, his face buried in his hands. "He's going to die, Mom. Do something."

Kitchen drawers slammed and John knocked over a chair on his way back to the family room. I looked up and saw him standing over us with a butcher knife in his hand.

"Oh my God, you could kill them with that thing."

"It's a risk we have to take. We're going to lose Tails if we don't try it." He slid the knife between the collar and Tail's neck and pushed down until the wide part of the blade sliced through the leather.

We watched as the collar released and dropped to the floor like a video in slow motion. Tails crumbled on the carpet in the midst of the debris. Sonic raced for the back porch.

"He thinks he did something wrong. Please, Dayton, go comfort him." I covered Tails with a blanket, picked him up and held him against my chest. His breath was warm on my neck. Kissing the top of his head, I carried him to the porch and sat with him in the rocker. "You're okay now, boy." I patted his back. "We need to get new collars today. Nylon with snap buckles."

John paced in the backyard, on his phone with the vet's office. Dayton sat on the grass with Sonic and ran his hands over his fur.

John finished talking to the vet and returned to the porch, tucking his phone in a back pocket. He said, "The lady at the vet's office said to look at his gums. If they aren't dark, he'll be okay."

He squatted in front of us and checked the puppy's mouth. Grinning, he ruffled Tails' head.

"They're pink," he said.

Susan Estomin Chappelear is an interior designer with an empty nest and a passion for writing. She started writing short stories and completed her first novel, *Skylar and The Daily Six Medallions,* middle grade fiction about emotionally challenged kids on an exciting journey of self-discovery. She also edits the newsletter, *Positive Thoughts for the Week,* and studies the craft of writing with Lynn Skapyak Harlin on The Shantyboat. She lives with her husband and rescue dog, Buddyman, in Jacksonville, Florida.

"A dog teaches a boy fidelity, perseverance, and to turn around three times before lying down." ~ *Robert Benchley*

Winnie
Photo courtesy of Even Guilford-Blake

A PIECE OF OUR LIVES' DELIGHT

Evan Guilford-Blake

I admit I was reluctant when my wife suggested we get a dog. We lead busy lives and I just wasn't sure either of us would make the time to give a four-legged pet the attention it needed and deserved.

We'd both had dogs as children, and we'd loved them, but as adults the only pets either of us had were our two ring-neck doves. We love them but, as a breed, doves are only slightly dumber than earthworms and only slightly better company than goldfish. They're the kinetic statuary of the pet world: Lovely to look at, delightful to hold, and as affectionate as zombies.

Still, Roxanna was adamant. "We have a small house but a large enclosed yard," she argued. "A small dog wouldn't demand the attention a large one would, and we could adopt a rescue, thus saving a dog's life and gaining a loving companion. After all," she reasoned, "we're getting older, we don't have kids. A pet would give us both an object of affection, and affection in return. Unconditional love."

"Okay," I said, with, nonetheless, a sigh.

"And, besides," Roxanna added, "it really won't want that much attention."

"Uh-huh. Right."

We began our search online in early fall, looking at dogs' pictures and histories. Then, on a pleasant Saturday morning, we visited several local pet supply stores that held monthly adoption events. The first and nearest one had a canine menagerie. Many were all or part Chihuahua, a breed I, who appreciates quiet, don't particularly like. They yip, loudly. One of our neighbors had one, and its bark can be heard from their yard at all hours. Even, sometimes, in our house.

We met a number of friendly and docile collies, spaniels and Lab mixes who panted charmingly for attention, tails aflutter, but they were larger than we were prepared to cope with. Roxanna wanted a full-fledged lap dog; that meant something under fifteen pounds, preferably under twelve.

Among those we met was a small mutt, obviously part terrier but just as obviously part something else. Several something elses, in fact. We'd seen Winnie's picture on the website of an agency called Small Dog Rescue, whose rep told us she'd been left, chained, inside a foreclosed house that had been abandoned. She'd tried to gnaw her way free, losing a number of teeth in the process. The county animal control agency found her, hair matted and skin ravaged by fleas.

Sensing she was gentle and potentially a good pet, they had turned her over to Small Dog Rescue. She'd been in a foster home with several other dogs for three months, during which time she'd been very well-behaved with both the humans and the other dogs.

I'd pointed out her photo early on to Roxanna, who agreed: She was tiny, with big eyes and a great smile. In the flesh, what there was of it, "skinny" was a major understatement. She was barely ten pounds, fluffy, white with a blonde strip along her back and, while willing to be held and petted, she was less than responsive. She licked my hand once but ignored Roxanna completely, except to look to her balefully.

Still, Winnie seemed, to me, to be *the* dog. She wasn't particularly outgoing but she was small, quiet, docile and obviously needy. And her full name was Winnie Words with Friends, a nice synchronicity. Both Roxanna and I are writers, and she is an avid Words with Friends player. "She's nice," Roxanna said, clearly unimpressed. "Let's look at the other places."

So we did. At both of them we saw more of the same: mixed-breed Chihuahuas, Jack Russells, Boston terriers and dachshunds. A dachshund had originally sparked Roxanna's interest in adopting, but it was another breed I was less than crazy about. Nor did I care for Pekinese, Pomeranians, or variations on a theme of Yorkshire terriers and other high-pitched yippers. We found a couple of small, outgoing terriers who were affectionate, but clearly high strung. They barked at everything and, in a couple of cases, were aggressive. One nipped at my hand when I tried to pet his face.

"He can be trained," the man in charge said. "It'll just take a couple weeks. I'd be glad to do it." We nodded.

"But," Roxanna said, "we don't want to take any chances." I agreed.

By this time we'd seen, petted, held, and scratched behind the ears of perhaps sixty dogs. Roxanna sighed.

"Why don't we take another look at Winnie?" I suggested. After all, Winnie was where we'd begun our search.

"Okay," she said, and shrugged. Winnie was still pretty passive.

"She's not very affectionate," Roxanna said.

"But she's quiet and she likes being held," I pointed out. Which was true. She went willingly from my arms to Roxanna's and back, lay on the ground belly up and wagged her tail enthusiastically when we scratched and petted her. She wouldn't eat a treat, but stared at us dolefully as we offered them. We later learned she didn't like to eat in public.

Finally, she licked Roxanna's hand.

That was three-and-a-half years ago. In the interim, we have taken to calling her our daughter, only half in jest. Winnie has come to be the queen of the household who graciously permits us to serve her every waking moment. She loves the car and goes with us almost everywhere, whether it's to the Post Office a mile away or to Gulf Shores, Alabama, a six-hour drive from our Atlanta home. Since Roxanna does all the driving, Winnie calmly inserts her now-twelve-pound self on my lap, and camps there for the duration, save for occasionally standing up to press her nose to the window or lick my arm. If Roxanna and I go out, Winnie's at the door to greet our return with excited whimpers, a flag-in-the-wind tail, and her own inimitable dance, for which she is amply rewarded with hugs, body scratches and belly rubs.

She knows it's bedtime when we turn off the television or our computers, or simply leave the couch. She scampers ahead of us, stops at the bedroom door and looks back, with an "I'm ready, where are *you*?" look on her face. Once we're in bed, she climbs up and approaches us, one at a time, for her good-night affection, which she returns by licking us until we insist she stop. Then she curls up and makes herself comfy. It's amazing, the amount of bed a twelve-pound dog can occupy!

The rest of the time? Well, she sleeps. Eighteen hours a day in one of her three beds. One is mobile, the others are in Roxanna's office and mine. Winnie lies there patiently while we work, then exuberantly follows us to the kitchen—dinner!; the back door—pee!; or outside—walk!; or on the sofa, between us while we read or watch a movie. She does deign to roll onto her back now and then, just to let us know her belly is available for a good rub, which we gladly bestow.

For us, there's a sense of well-being that comes with doing it, a sense of bonding that must be what it's like to bond with your child. The surrogation Winnie provides is both a peace and a piece of our lives' delight.

Evan Guilford-Blake writes poetry, prose and plays for adults and children. His novel *Noir(ish)* is published by Penguin. Holland House issued his short story collection *American Blues* in October 2014, and Verto Publishing will publish his collection *Love & Loss & Love* in January 2016. Thirty-one of his plays are also published. He and his wife (and inspiration) Roxanna, a healthcare writer and jewelry designer, live in the southeastern U.S., with Winnie Words (the subject of "A Piece of Our Lives' Delight") and their two dumb-as-dirt (but lovable) ring-neck doves, Quill and Gabriella.

Winnie
Photo courtesy of Evan Guilford-Blake

Ace
Photo Courtesy of Lori Taylor

ACE

Lori Taylor

It was September 1986. Before we even had our bed set up in our new house, we went to the local animal shelter to look for a puppy. We weren't allowed to have pets in our first apartment, but now we were moving into a house where we could have the dog I'd always wanted.

The lady at the shelter said eleven puppies had been found in a dumpster. Based on their markings, she guessed they were a collie and German shepherd mix. That sounded like they were going to grow up to be bigger dogs than we had wanted to adopt, but they were so cute, I couldn't resist taking a peek.

When she opened the kennel door, all the puppies backed away from us, cowering in the corner. Except one. He did that little roly-poly puppy run/waddle over to where I had crouched down. He put his front paws up on my leg, as if to say, "I choose you!"

How could I say no?

Thinking he would grow to be a big beast, we wanted to choose a macho name for him. We considered King, Rex and Max, but finally settled on Ace. Despite our concerns, Ace grew to only about knee high on me, and he never weighed more than forty-two pounds. Our vet thought he might have some border collie and/or English shepherd in him.

As a puppy, Ace was not kind to any box of Kleenex left within his reach, and shoes were considered his personal chew toys for a while. When he was very young he was traumatized by the neighbor's huge cat, which swiped his nose with its claws more than once.

We moved from the house to an acreage, where we had lots of outside cats. Ace usually avoided them as much as he could, but the kittens would follow him around and we could almost see him roll his eyes when they snuggled up to him as he was resting in the shade.

He was smart and playful, and extremely intuitive. He knew when I wanted him to snuggle with me, and he knew when he should just lie down next to me, instead of on me.

Ace was very attentive through both my pregnancies, and with the arrival of our first daughter, I think Ace thought she was his baby. If she cried and I didn't immediately run to her, Ace would come to get me. And if anyone else wanted to hold his baby, he would allow them to, but he never took his eyes off of her.

When I was pregnant with our second daughter, and Ace was nearly twelve years old, we learned that he had cancer in his throat and in his colon. The vet assured us he wasn't in any pain yet, but we monitored him closely.

May 5, 1999, about two and a half weeks after the baby was born, I was up for an early morning feeding. Ace came over to where I was sitting, and he just stared at me. The look in his eyes was almost scary. I'd never seen that expression on him before.

I told him, "It's ok, Ace. Go lay down."

He went into the other room and lay down, but started to bleed. By the time my husband got him to town, he was gone. I felt he'd stuck around to make sure everything was ok with the baby, and then he was ready to let go.

We've had other dogs, but I have a hard time being patient with them sometimes because they're not Ace. Fifteen years later, his picture still sits in our bedroom and my office.

Twelve years with Ace was not enough.

Although Ace was their first and their favorite, **Lori Taylor** and her husband, Steve, have adopted seven shelter dogs over the years. Steve and Lori live in Spencer, Iowa, with their younger daughter Maren; their older daughter Liz and her husband, Scott Thompson, live in Forest City, Iowa. Steve and Lori celebrated their 30th wedding anniversary in the fall of 2015.

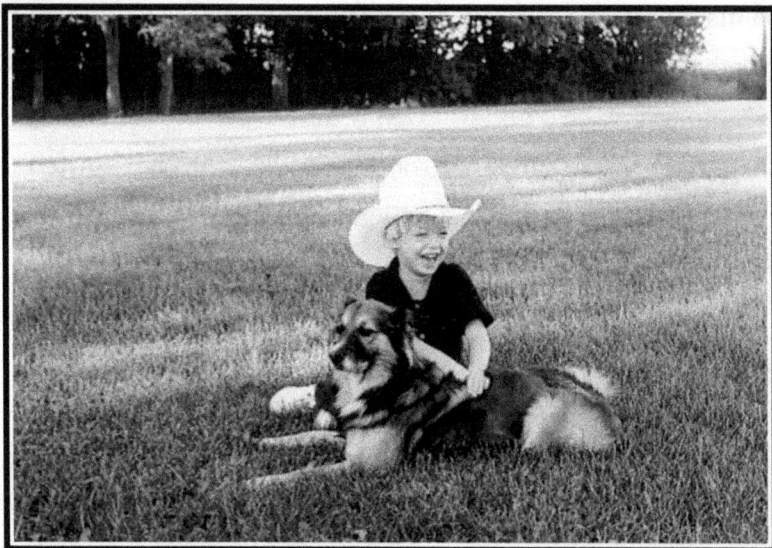

Ace & Liz
Photo courtesy of Lori Taylor

"Outside of a dog, a book is a man's best friend. Inside of a dog it's too dark to read." ~ *Groucho Marx*

THE END

THE END

SEND US YOUR STORY

Shapato Publishing LLC is gathering stories for the next "Rescue Anthology." I you have a story about an animal you rescued, and which as a result became a valued member of your or someone else's family, please consider submitting it to us. Photos are also very welcome.

Word Count: 500 – 1200 (with a little flexibility)

SEND STORIES TO:

Mail: Shapato Publishing LLC
        PO # 476
        Everly, IA 51338

EMail: jean@shapatopublishing.com

We look forward to hearing from you!

Jean Tennant
Shapato Publishing, LLC